FALLING INTO FREEDOM

My Journey from the Edge
to Find Personal Freedom

Janie

From my heart, I send you all the love you deserve. May you always Be Well...

Michael Doud

FALLING INTO FREEDOM

Copyright © 2018 by Michael Doud

Cover photo permitted by an Extended License from PhotoMarket
through Creative Market of San Francisco. ID # - 77107579

Printed in the United States of America
First Printing, 2018

ISBN 978-1-7326117-0-2

www.michaeldoud.com

michael@michaeldoud.com

To Michelle
For teaching me about unconditional love.

Contents

Acknowledgments

I am grateful to so many people for their friendship, guidance, support, and critical input that assisted me in making this longtime dream come to life.

To my wife Burr Leonard, I'm profoundly grateful to you for taking the time to read and re-read this manuscript providing essential guidance along with your best effort to teach me punctuation, grammar, and transitions. I was a poor student in high school, and I'm still a poor student; so, all errors belong to me. Your willingness to continue to push on my resistance was sublime.

To John Poppy, I bow with profound humbling thanks. Your editing and soft prodding helped to shape this manuscript into something I'm willing to make public. Your kindness and skills are beyond words.

To Christopher Titmuss, your love of The Beatles, the dharma, and probing dialogue during retreats you led, enhanced my life tremendously. Through our imperfections and clarity, we are brothers still taking steps on this journey. Thank you.

To Christina Feldman with Christopher, you founded Gaia House in West Ogwell, England. I can think of no better place in this world to participate in a personal retreat. The support given in this beautifully rustic center is truly divine. You guided me for the most potent ninety days of my life. I can only bow to you with honor, grace, and gratitude.

To Jack Kornfield, it is from your dharma talks, your one-on-one guidance in times of personal strife, and your one-word instruction, that I feel blessed for having had the opportunity to know you. I am awed by what you've done to lead westerners to learn more about the truth, as it is. You've shared all this using your path with heart.

Additionally, I want to gratefully acknowledge Katie Swanson for her very detailed notes and thoughts. Lastly, I'm deeply indebted to Mimi Fleischman,

Bruce Herrmann, Gabrielle Woods, Clark Melrose, Noelle Oxenhandler, and Steve Graber for wading through original drafts and taking time to share what worked and what didn't work.

To all the others, regardless of the type of relationship we've had, those who know me or have interacted with me through the years, you have helped me see myself and have become part of who I am. For your presence to help shape my life and this story, with appreciation, I am of gratitude.

Note: In this book, *Falling into Freedom*, I've done my best to recount my life as accurately as possible. All the incidents in this book happened. I've not included the last names of individuals except specific teachers from whom I've been grateful enough to learn. I've written from my notes and memory. Please accept my sincere apologies to those who experienced these events differently.

Preface

In the winter of 1989, on a windy cliff overlooking the Pacific Ocean, it hit me. I was depressed and had been for nearly all of my 38 years. Looking down at the churning sea, I considered ending my life right there. My only other option was to change it, completely. *Falling into Freedom* is the story of the amazing, crazy, and revealing adventures that began after I stepped back from the cliff and initiated my search for the wisdom that would set me free.

This story is about my quest for freedom, personal freedom, the kind that would allow me to see things as they are and not as I would want them to be. During this journey, I revisited my upbringing, the successes, and failures of my teens, killing human beings in Vietnam, and drug abuse. I also had to acknowledge that despite my love of being a dad, I'd had two failed marriages and had countless failed relationships. I needed to find a way to understand and account for all my actions.

The Buddha once said, "No one saves us but ourselves. No one can no one may. We ourselves must walk the path." I took this to mean I had to find my truth. This story shares my challenging 9-year journey of reviewing my past while pushing myself through difficult internal and external trials to understand the importance of learning to see, accept, and embrace my life's curriculum.

The path I took included training to become a personal growth seminar teacher while augmenting this training by reading influential philosophical and spiritual books. I expanded my daily meditation practice which cumulated in identifying my five principles for personal freedom. The story ends in 1998, at a silent meditation center in England where I sat in silence for ninety days.

Chapter 1

Monsters

I zipped up the tent flap, slipped into my sleeping bag, and closed my eyes. It was my first time camping alone on the rugged Big Sur Coast of California. I was in a great place to get away from the city, my career, self-obsession, and figure out, at the age of 38, what the hell was going on with my life. Great place, yes. Great idea—until I heard the monster sniffing around just outside my flimsy pup tent.

I prayed the beast wouldn't claw through the thin fabric and see me as its next meal. The arrival of danger on this cold, windy night, my helplessness, my idiocy…, hit hard. I lay there listening for every snapped twig, every whisper of the wind, every grunt through a fanged snout.

Nervously, I backtracked through my thoughts and tried to figure out where I had gone wrong in selecting this site at Andrew Molera State Park. I wanted seclusion, a quiet place to meditate and get myself together. So here I was in a completely vacant beachside campground more than two miles away from the nearest help. Other campers had the good sense to stay away in winter when storms can roll down from the Pacific Northwest to slam against the beautifully massive cliffs of Big Sur. I tried to put a name to the monster by remembering the signs at the visitors' center warning campers about raccoons, coyotes, and bobcats. I must have overlooked the sign for bears, mountain lions, and wolves.

A thought hit me. I've done this before. I'm doing it again, making yet another attempt to escape my unsatisfactory life and probably botching it one more time. I let out a half-laugh at the insight. Was the monster I was envisioning bigger and more carnivorous than any real one? Did the beast I was so afraid of really exist or was I hearing the echo of a reoccurring pitfall? My lifelong habit of turning my back on situations that didn't meet my standards or expectations that usually landed me in trouble. My trip to Big Sur was supposed to be a retreat during which I would have space and solitude to mull over my dissatisfaction with my existence as a small cog within the corporate world and why I wasn't getting any new opportunities. It was February of 1989. Although it hadn't crossed my mind the week before that I would be camping; I did have a feeling that something in my life was going to change, and soon.

The fear of the beast outside, mixed with the cold wind of winter, pushed me deeper into reflections of disenchantment and my sleeping bag. Usually, I dealt with such feelings by distancing myself from the object of my disappointment. Whether it was a girlfriend, job, family, or life, I would start pulling my energy in towards myself and hold on for dear life as I spiraled down a well of darkness until one day something would shift and I would start to climb back up to something new. However, right now there was nowhere to run or hide.

Just five months earlier, in September, the company I worked for had gone bankrupt. I couldn't believe it. I'd finally found a job that I liked. Good people, useful product, opportunities… my life was about to unfold. I was Director of Management Information Systems for the company, which had developed and was going into production with a cutting-edge wristwatch paging and communication device. I had stock options. Life was going along according to my latest plan. Everything was finally falling into place. But the invention was ahead of its time, and the company failed.

Everyone except those on the C-level executive team was laid off. However, because the rent was paid, we were told we could keep our offices and use our desks, computers and photocopy machines for "as long as the lights are burning." So, I simply kept getting up in the morning and going to work. All through October, November, December, and January, I would go into the office and go through the process of looking for work. I'd made hundreds of telephone calls, set appointments, and met with the people I believed held the key to my next job. There was nothing left to do but wait, and this was very hard because I was impatient and wanted results now. I despised waiting for someone else's judgment of me to match my own. I wanted someone to say, "We want you."

One day while sitting in the office it hit me, maybe there was some deeper meaning to this course of events. Perhaps I was striking out on these job opportunities for some more substantial cosmic reason. Maybe I was colliding with a divine plan in the universe. Was I bumping up against a sign pointing to another life path for me? What I did know is that I felt alone, very alone, and most of all disenchanted with the way my life had gone thus far.

I already had two failed marriages behind me, and I wasn't meeting compatible partners. I never seemed to have enough money, and until this last job, I had little joy in the work I was doing. I felt sentenced to disappointment in all avenues of my life, and now this, jobless and nothing on the horizon.

Just one short week ago, on Tuesday, Valentine's Day, February 14th, I was sitting at my desk when the idea of going camping popped into my head. I burst out laughing. Somebody down the hall hollered, "What's so funny?" I shouted back, "I've decided to hell with all this. I'm going camping." I felt downright giddy. Another co-worker chimed in to say he would lend me his pup tent if I needed it. With his tent and my stove, sleeping bag, and other camping supplies, I was ready for what I suddenly knew was going to be my next step.

Now, lying in the moonless dark of night, listening to the ravenous beast prowling outside my tent, I found myself begging God for mercy. I asked Him to lay His divine hand upon my life and make everything the way I wanted it. First and foremost, I wished for some peace along with freedom from fear of the monster. A little security and safety would be excellent. But my prayers brought no relief. My panic and fear blended into total confusion. I was lost and wanted to die. I thought my life might very well end right here on this empty beach.

Random thoughts flew by. How on earth did I get to this point? Is this what all my best efforts in life had added up to? Would my gravestone say, "He ended up as a quivering bowl of Jell-O?" Or maybe even better, "He was dinner." I had hoped my life would have been more like my inner vision, which included being married to a beautiful woman, a large house, cars, and financial success: the satisfaction of having made it.

I don't know how long I lay there begging God for mercy, but what I do know is that this night began a change that would transform the rest of my life because the monster outside my tent might have been me.

Chapter 2

Sticks

Despite being frightened out of my mind while lying in my tent, I must have gotten some sleep because I startled myself awake. Jerking up, I turned on my flashlight and looked at my watch: 5:30 a.m. and still dark outside. I listened intently for any sound of the monster. Nothing. "God, I made it through the night," I said aloud to myself. Now what? I decided to look outside and survey my campsite for damage the monster might have done.

Poking my head outside the tent flap, I peered through the darkness, listening, ready to leap back into the safety of my tent. Nothing. Barely any sound at all. Clouds obscured the stars, the wind had quieted down, and there seemed to be only the slow movement of an early winter morning.

"I guess I'm safe for another day," I mumbled out loud.

I sat up on my sleeping bag, my head touching the condensation that had accumulated on the inside of the tent during the night and thought about what to do next. Get up, and stand up to my fears by taking back the campground? Go back to sleep with a slightly improved sense of security? None of these options sounded good, so I decided to sit and meditate while waiting for the light of day.

The problem was, every time I tried to focus on my breath and put last night's monster out of my mind, I found fear lurking inside my body, twisting my gut into a knot. Time and again the frustration of not finding peace, but instead unrelenting apprehension, created an acute feeling of disappointment. After forty-five minutes, I gave up, resigned to sit there and wait for daybreak.

Dawn found me looking around the campground for telltale signs of my nighttime visitor. The muddy claw marks on my ice chest were proof that my fears were founded. However, the fact that my plastic ice chest had survived the rampage of the fanged monster indicated that my perception of its size, shape, and power was probably a bit exaggerated. Raccoon, I thought with a slightly chagrined sense of relief.

The previous day, while driving through the village of Big Sur, I had noticed some private campgrounds advertising hot showers. The thought lifted my spirits. After taking a sip of cold water from my canteen, I secured my campsite and walked down the trail illuminated by the early morning light to my car.

I found the showers easily enough, and as the warm water spilled over my body, an immense wave of relief flowed through my entire being. Wonderful!

Driving past the campsite registration office, I stopped and slid a couple of dollars under the window to pay for the water I'd used. God, I felt good.

Back at the campground, I was invigorated and ready to eat something. The thought of a cup of coffee and hot noodles in broth lifted my spirits. As I washed down the last of the noodles with my third cup of coffee, I decided I needed to gather firewood for nighttime and morning campfires. So off I went in search of wood.

I walked through an open meadow toward a more forested area about a quarter mile away. After crossing a small stream on a log, I found a leaf-covered trail that headed towards a small forest of trees. I stopped under their canopy and breathed the moist, dense, fragrant air.

As I bent down to pick up another piece of wood, I suddenly saw how I was choosing each stick. I would pick up one that was "good enough" and then drop it for another seemingly better piece. I did this repeatedly. I began to watch myself do this from some other place inside me. It was as if there were two people walking in the same body: the person gathering wood and the person watching the person gathering wood. The part of me watching all this started thinking about the person who was picking up sticks of wood and dropping them for more perfect sticks. That person, I thought, was stupid.

A wave of sadness came over me with the realization that my life seemed filled with this endless search for the more perfect thing. Whether it was a job, a place to live, or a relationship with a woman, I seemed always to be looking for something better than what I had.

I felt my stomach tighten. "Is this true?" I asked myself.

I started to get defensive. Isn't finding something "better" superior to accepting what I had? Isn't being dissatisfied with one's current situation the basis for advancing one's life? I recalled a talk by a motivational speaker, Gunther Klaus, who quoted George Bernard Shaw, "The reasonable man adapts himself to the world: the unreasonable one persists in trying to adapt the world to suit himself. Therefore, all progress depends on the unreasonable man." Recalling my past, I would say I had been the unreasonable man always pushing for something different, something new. Isn't that how most people in society advance their lives?

On the other hand, many sources of wisdom teach us to "Accept what is." I had been told that when we accept what is currently in our life, we make way for a truly transformative level of change and growth. This is completely different from trying to force change. What if true change comes from a natural evolutionary process? Again, my defensive nature sprang up, insisting, "I'm in charge of my life, and I want to change because I'm dissatisfied!" Then I remembered a therapist I saw during the struggles of my first marriage telling me, "Power is defensivelessness." I took this to mean that in being defensive, I give up my power, and I wanted to be empowered. My thoughts kept volleying between these ideas until I told myself, with a light sense of relief, "I need to pay attention to this dialogue."

My day-to-day existence was far from either of these ideals. I was neither imposing my power because I was defensive nor was I surrendering in acceptance. Right there in that grove of trees, I was witnessing how my mind would argue and be defensive about changes and decisions I had made, and how I always had justifications for my actions at the tip of my tongue. In one thing I was consistent: I wanted to change, and I wanted it to be a certain way. I desired a job that I loved, a relationship I cherished, to be healthy enough to do what I wanted, enough money to buy what I wanted, and internal peace and freedom. Why not? My version of how the world *should be* was so much better than what was actually happening.

Witnessing this pattern of behavior reflected in the simple process of picking up wood brought me to laughter. It was not that selecting a particular piece of wood for the fire wasn't a good thing to do. It was the absurdity of my compelling and chronic dissatisfaction with the wood that was so absurd. With sticks of wood, work, or relationships, I would always find myself looking around for something different from what I had. This cycle seemed endless.

After stacking my chosen wood at the campground, I decided to hike along one of the many trails in Big Sur to reflect further on this insight. On a map, the path appeared to have woods and open meadows, with views overlooking the inland hills and, at its farthest reach, the cliffs and shoreline. I packed a simple lunch of cheese, water, half a baguette, an apple, and granola bars and set off along the trail.

As I walked along the trail, the morning's revelation kept cropping up in my head. Was I *always* looking for something different from what I had? Was I still looking for something just over the horizon or around the corner? What was I looking for anyway? While asking these questions, I checked in with my body to see how it felt. Did I still feel as if I had a hole in the middle of my stomach?

Yes.

And while I was paying attention to this emptiness, another sensation appeared, the feeling of wanting to cry. I realized, yet again, that my life was just an endless stream of wanting the next thing and never being satisfied with what was there now. The corners of my mouth fell, as tears ran down my cheeks. Wiping away the tears, I deliberately shut the door on what I was thinking.

Up the hill I went, paying attention to the world around me: birds flying overhead, insects on the edge of the trail, plants with their infinite variety of patterns and colors, all creating ways for me to ignore what I was feeling. Cresting a small ridge, I came upon a small grove of pine trees, and again the smell of pine resin, damp leaves, and moist ground filled the air. It was now late morning and time for a short rest. I decided that this might be an excellent place to meditate, so I looked for a place to sit.

The energy of the space surrounded by these beautiful trees and the quiet of the hills seemed ideal to sit with my questions. As I settled into meditation, feeling my breath as it passed across the edges of my nostrils, my pent-up anxiousness gradually left my stomach. With each out-breath, I became a little quieter inside.

I became conscious of the noise of the wind passing through the leaves and needles of the trees. "Hearing," I said aloud, noting what my mind was paying attention to. The moisture in the air felt cool on my cheeks. "Sensing," I said quietly to myself. After another fifteen minutes, the stillness of my body reflected a quiet remembering of more peaceful times. "Remembering," I whispered to myself. My breathing became all I was aware of, and my mind stopped thinking. I was merely sitting in the forest, breathing.

After about an hour, I reached over to my daypack and pulled out the apple. The crackling sound of my bite into its dark, red skin echoed through the trees. Its taste and crispness brought a smile. At this moment, I did not need to look for anything more perfect.

Getting up, I immediately noticed a beautiful and peaceful clarity in the movement of my walking. I looked up the trail, started to take some steps, and felt each muscle in my legs engage as I placed one foot in front of the other. Lift, move, place, and roll my weight to the other foot. My movement was so exact, so precise. With each step, I could feel the clarity of this motion. I felt my breathing in my diaphragm and the coolness around my nostrils. I felt in sync with the world.

After hiking for another couple of hours, I reached the summit of the hill. The trail turned right and headed down an open, grassy hillside meadow bordered by a fence meandering down towards the cliff edge above the ocean. From this vantage point, I could see miles up and down the coastline. The demarcation line between the deep-blue-gray ocean and jagged cliffs was clearly defined, with each element staking its territory with grandeur. It was nearly 1:00 p.m. and I thought this would be an excellent place to stop, rest, and have some of the cheese, bread, and water I had brought for lunch.

But when I sat on a fallen log and felt the brisk, crisp wind coming in off the ocean, I started to feel alone, empty again. Thinking I could zip up my jacket to stop my shivering body did little good. The shaking was coming from within, the reminder about my frustration of not having the answers to my life. The shaking, in turn, created a pounding in my head like Taiko drums. With each beat of the drum, my sad separation from the world around me intensified. Anger arose and spoke to me with agitated speed, while the hurt of rejection and non-acceptance of my life, as it was currently playing out, fought for my attention and consolation. All the while, the wind that was colliding with my face helped to dry my falling tears and kept me painfully aware of how my heart was breaking.

To distract myself and stop the deep-seated pain, I opened my daypack and pulled out the rest of my food. Barely tasting the food, I sensed it sliding into my stomach, providing exceptional comfort to my body. The nourishment almost immediately changed how I was feeling. I began to regain some of my composure. Then a question arose from deep within me. It would be the most important question I had ever asked myself. The question was, "Am I happy?"

I had asked this question before, many times, but the difference this time was the place within me from which the problem arose. The issue was no longer about the kind of momentary happiness one feels when they've just received a raise at work, when they've met a new girlfriend or boyfriend, or when one welcomes a new baby. It was as if my whole mind, body, and soul were simultaneously asking me to take stock of everything I'd ever felt, said, or done.

The sensation might have been like the experience people have when they are near death and see their life flash in front of them. Only, I wasn't dying. I was facing the accumulation of all my life's actions and asking myself, "Who am I? Am I happy with what I see?"

Again, tears started to well up in my eyes, and my body began to shake with the fear of truth. At first a hesitant "no" bubbled up to the surface, but then I could feel myself getting defensive and starting to think my way out of letting this deeper answer surface. "This isn't about right now," I said to myself, feeling myself surrender to the deeper truth beginning to arise from within, "This is about my whole life." I asked the question again, "Am I happy with my life?" The answer came powerfully from deep within me. It was a clear, definite "No."

Chapter 3

Love-ins and Meditation

The stark realization and deep, truthful response to the question brought additional tears that the cold sea breeze coming off the ocean dried as quickly as they came making my cheeks feel tight. I was turning 39 this year and admitting to myself that I was unhappy with my life continued to push its impact deeper into my soul. "What happened to my life?" I wondered. The more I thought about it; the more it hurt.

I yelled out towards the ocean to no one in particular, maybe to a God, "What did I do wrong?"

I wanted to medicate myself as the sadness crawled around inside my body. It was the sadness of not having the kind of life I had envisioned for myself. I had hoped to have embodied inner peace, not inner anguish.

Instead, for all the work I'd done, both inside and out, here I was sitting on a log in a meadow feeling that I'd betrayed myself.

Part of me wanted to shut out this new awareness. I imagined that if I were home in Pleasant Hill in San Francisco's East Bay, I'd turn on the television, drink a few beers, eat some tortilla chips, and distract myself in some way. Sitting in my easy chair, I'd pick up the remote control and press buttons and watch two or three programs at the same time or maybe find a single show that interested me enough to sit through.

The reality was that I was sitting on the log, staring out at the ocean, my heart and mind feeling very heavy. Knowing that meditation often assisted me in being able to let go of internal turmoil, I gently closed my eyes and paid attention to my breathing.

As I sipped the cold wind through my nostrils, thoughts about meditation, how it came into my life, and my path to this moment flooded my mind.

I discovered meditation in 1967 at a love-in at Irvine Park in Orange County, California, when I was 17 years old. These love-ins were held every couple of months and did not appear to be organized by any one person or group. A flyer would appear on a telephone pole or a public poster board, like the one at the Costa Mesa Teen Center, telling people when and where the next event would take place. Or someone would tell friends, "There's a love-in next Saturday, do you wanna go?"

The love-ins appeared to grow organically, and they took on a life of their own. My friends and I would get together at a convenient location, fill up a couple of cars or my friend Randy T.'s old Excelsior Dairy truck or a VW microbus with people, and head out. Along the way, we'd stop at a roadside orange stand and purchase a couple of big bags of oranges so that we would have something to pass out to the people we'd meet during our walks through the brightly dressed crowd.

When Irvine Park was the venue, I liked to walk counter-clockwise on one of the circular roads, stopping to accept free food, drink, and the good smoke while passing out my oranges. It felt so good to be a participant in gatherings that were a symbol of societal change. It seemed counter to the established culture of the time, and this alone made the love-ins important.

This new approach to being human was notably different from my strict upbringing. My brother, most of my friends, and I were brought up believing we had to work hard for everything we wanted. The love-in idea of free-form giving and receiving with a generous, loving spirit was not part of our culture. For generations in my family, nothing was given to anyone without a price. I received a full-sized, 26-inch bicycle for Christmas when I was seven years old along with a comment: "This is the last bicycle we'll ever buy you, so take care of it. If you lose this one or want another one, you'll have to buy it yourself." I know that these statements weren't meant to be harsh or callous, but rather to underscore the nature of the bike as a gift. It was bought with hard-earned money sacrificed from something else, and I needed to take care of the present. We had very little money, and because of this, the gift came with conditions.

In contrast, the experience of being with a large group of colorful, smiling people who were practicing the art of giving something away without requiring something in return was new to me. I liked the feeling of carrying around the big bag of oranges and handing them to anyone I wanted. Sometimes I would receive something in return and sometimes I wouldn't. It never mattered. What mattered was the giving.

On this day, I had set my bag of oranges down, and I was wandering around when a young woman with a very slight build and curly long blond hair came up and handed me a glass dish of tapioca pudding. Mesmerized by her brightly colored top and long purple skirt, I received it gratefully, and we parted ways. As I ate the last of the pudding, I started thinking about the bowl and the silver spoon she had handed me. How will I return it to her? Where will I put it? Will she miss it later? Does it mean something to her? I came across a drinking fountain where I took a drink and washed the dish and spoon. I continued my journey through the park and found that

I was approaching a large crowd gathering to see a magician. Suddenly, just as in a Hollywood film, I found myself face to face with the owner of the dish and spoon. With joy in my heart, I smiled at my luck while handing them to her and saying, "Thank you." The wide grin on her face told me how pleased she was to have them back and clean, as well.

After relocating my bag of oranges, I continued wandering through the park giving them out to anyone who wanted to receive one. Before long, I came across a small group in a meadow. The crowd seemed to be just starting to gather, and my curiosity took over. I saw a slight, clear-eyed guy dressed in a light white gauzy material with what looked like an Indian headscarf. In a very loose and laid-back way, he was asking people if they wanted to experience *meditation* by inviting them to sit in a circle. As people walked by, some joined us in this circle, and it grew until more than one hundred people were sitting in a huge circle.

The meditation teacher began giving instructions on how to sit. He told us to ground ourselves on the grass with our backs straight, legs crossed, hands gently resting in our laps, and eyes either closed or gazing downward, all the while reminding us to focus on our breathing. All of us shifted our bodies accordingly, and before I knew it, the whole group fell into silence. Every so often the teacher would encourage us by saying "Let go of the thought you are having," and "Return your focus to the breath." We sat like this for 40 to 50 minutes before he said, "Gently bring your awareness back to the group."

I did not have an extraordinary experience while we were meditating, and quite frankly, I was disappointed. I was hoping to be swept away in a wave of total awe, wonderment, and possibly enlightenment. "Hell," I thought. I was hoping to be fully enlightened by this one experience. I'd expected to have metamorphosed into my perception of the Maharishi Mahesh Yogi, who had recently come into the awareness of many because of The Beatles association with him.

I did notice how quiet my body and mind seemed while the group sat beaming at each other. But then my insecurities blundered forth as I started wondering if everyone else in the group had experienced enlightenment and I hadn't. Looking again around the circle, I was relieved to find that everyone also seemed to have the same subdued look about them that I had! Almost immediately my anxiousness subsided, and although I wasn't enlightened, I felt as though I'd been transported to a place of quiet, peace, openness, and a more extensive caring for humanity.

After a few more minutes of gazing about our circle, the teacher announced that we were going to practice another form of meditation that included chanting the word "Aum." This word or sound, he explained, was the most sacred symbol and sound in Hindu *dharma* ("the truth" and "as it is"). *Aum* was the sound of the infinite or the essence of the entire universe.

The teacher asked each of us to maintain our current sitting positions and to open our palms slightly to our sides, putting our right palm facing downward and our left palm facing upward. Then we were to touch our neighbor's open and extended palms gently. Therefore, my downward facing right-hand palm was lightly resting on the left upward facing palm of the neighbor on my right. On the other side, my upward facing left palm rested on my neighbor's downward facing right palm. The one critical instruction was not to grasp the other person's hand. Now all of us in the circle was connected.

We all took one in-breath, and during the out-breath, we said "Aum" extending the word for as long as we had breath. At first, all of us were trying to coordinate our in-breath and out-breaths, saying "Aum" at the same time. However, we were guided to follow our pattern and, in doing so, the resulting "Aum" never stopped. It became a continuous ever-present tone.

Not long after this exercise began, I felt a surge of energy coming through my right hand and up my arm, through my right shoulder, up into my head where it completed a half circle, headed down my left side, and out my left palm. The strength of this energy was beyond anything I had ever experienced before. It was as if someone had plugged me into a generator producing a powerful and benevolent flow of energy, almost like hugging electricity. It was connecting me to the essence of love in each person in the circle. It was like seeing and feeling the best of each person through this constant flow of energy. It was, without a doubt, the first time I had ever felt I was completely and wholly part of a group. I was part of each person sitting in the circle because something of them flowed through me. The funny thing was I didn't know any of them, yet it felt as if we were one person. It was amazing.

When this session ended, I realized I had been part of something I would carry with me through my entire life. I'd touched the divine energy of spirit, the one residing within and outside each of us. We had all connected as one. It was at that moment; I knew that meditation would become part of my life and would help me to navigate the road ahead.

Chapter 4

Dazed and Confused

Although I had a moving experience during that meditation session, it was fleeting and hard to recreate. With no one else to assist me, reconstructing inner peace, if even for a moment, seemed futile.

Despite that glimpse into the power of meditation, it was clear to me that I was lost. Part of me wanted to be enlightened. My recent experiences in meditation, love-ins in Southern California, and multiple visits to San Francisco gave me a taste of freedoms one can experience by living a free-flowing, more open, less money-oriented way of life. This part of me, the seeker for inner peace, joy, and happiness was pulling at me mainly because of the upheavals in our country. Becoming part of a growing wave of people who were less concerned about money and things just felt right.

Another part of me wanted to join the revolutionary movement that focused on changing what was wrong with our country. The Yippies, (the newly formed Youth International Party), were significant drivers of the campaign. This group founded by Abbie Hoffman, Jerry Rubin, Anita Hoffman, Nancy Kurshan, and Paul Krassner translated countercultural ideals into action; they had engineered a noteworthy disruption of the 1968 Democratic Convention in Chicago.

Then there was the third part of me that just wanted to work, make some money, and go to rock concerts, smoke pot, drop LSD, and live on my own.

In sum, I had to choose among three directions for my life: Become a free spirit, become an activist and stand up against the current social structure, or work and be "responsible" and along the way make money and enjoy the fruits of my labor. These choices wrestled inside me with no resolution in sight. On top of this, there was the indecisive way I was currently living, chameleon-like, fitting in with whatever group I was hanging with, not noticed or seen. I wasn't standing up for myself, just wondering what was next. The truth is, I was nowhere. It's why I loved the song "Nowhere Man" by The Beatles.

But I was at least debating my choices. Supporting the first choice were my desires for freedom, non-structure, and joy, which came from my trips to San Francisco and the love-ins in Southern California. The second choice seemed more difficult for me because it would mean defiantly standing up for something and possibly jail time. Although I participated in an anti-war march in Hollywood, and a few protesters were arrested for property destruction, I had felt out of my element. As for the third choice, I had already been going down this path since age 12.

That year, I remembered what was told to me on that Christmas morning at age seven, and I decided it was time for me to earn money so that I could buy what I wanted. What I wanted was a new 10-speed, metallic light-blue Schwinn bicycle. Knowing my dad could always use someone to sweep up the floor and be an inexpensive general laborer at the fiberglass product manufacturing company he was a partner in, I asked him for work. Simultaneously, I also got a paper route delivering *The Daily Pilot* in our Costa Mesa neighborhood.

My first goal was to work as much as possible to get the new bike I'd eyed at the Schwinn store and then save up until I was fifteen and a half years old for a motorcycle.

It didn't take long to save up the $65.00 for the new bike, and in short order, I was ready to take on a new job to save up for the motorcycle.

During my sophomore year of high school, I got myself a job at Der Wienerschnitzel, a fast food hot dog restaurant. Soon I was the manager of a store on Harbor Boulevard in Costa Mesa. Ruben G., who owned this store and another less than a mile away in the same town on 17th Street, was negotiating for an additional one in neighboring Huntington Beach. I knew he'd need strong help, and my trait of being very meticulous and responsible made me an excellent fit for him. I enjoyed working for Ruben because he immediately saw my strengths and willingness to take charge and be responsible. Demonstrating his faith, he started letting me do inventory, order products, and make the chili for the chili dogs. Then he asked for my feedback when he hired someone and began allowing me to develop the store scheduling. When he asked me to join him in the interview process, I felt I had become his right-hand man.

For taking on these responsibilities, Ruben paid me three times the minimum wage of $1.25 an hour. At age 15, I was embodying the family tradition of working hard to get ahead. Right on schedule, at 15 ½, I bought a used yellow Yamaha motorcycle. It allowed me to get to and from work and school faster, and the freedom I felt having my motorized transportation was terrific.

I would get up, shower, get dressed, and eat something for breakfast, usually cereal. Then with joy in my heart, I'd head to the garage and roll out my yellow Yamaha to the driveway. Climbing aboard the Yamaha, lifting myself on my right foot I'd engage the kick-starter and get a thrill hearing the engine come to life and knowing that in a few moments I'd be rolling down the street. As the wind collided with my face and blew through my hair, I was away from everyone. The only important thing was riding in freedom.

Six months later, on July 26, 1966, the day after I got my automobile drivers license, I put a down payment on a dark blue, 1965 VW Variant-S and made monthly payments for one year to pay it off.

During the summer before my senior year of high school, it was clear that I had opted for my third life choice, the traditional path, and admittedly the easiest because it was the one I was already on. I started a job as a welder's apprentice at a company called SAMPCO (Santa Ana Metal Products Company) in Santa Ana, California. I worked part-time from Noon to 5:00 p.m. because I was only going to school until 11:15 a.m. It was a great job because it made me, still a high-school student, a lot of money. After taxes, I was bringing home more than $175.00 a week. For a 17-year-old in 1967-68, when gas was around 30 cents a gallon and cigarettes about 25 cents a pack, this was fantastic.

As spring came and went and summer drew near, however, the heat under the welding helmet became intense. The work was dirty and hard especially when I was using the grinder to clean up welds. I began to feel trapped by the closed confines and limited view of the world that I could see only through the little rectangular glass lens of my welding helmet, a world framed by the welding beads I was laying down and by my growing concern for what kind of life I could expect from doing this for a living.

In my free time, I still dipped into the hippie revolution, attended love-ins, traveled to San Francisco, and marched on Hollywood Boulevard against the war. However, my favorite way to spend my hard-earned money was to go to rock concerts to see my favorite totally far-out and heavy bands of the 1960s. I think I saw them all except for The Beatles and The Rolling Stones.

In addition to the famous groups, I also saw and heard a few of the up-and-coming San Francisco bands of the '60s including the Jefferson Airplane and

Quicksilver Messenger Service. I went to their performances with adoration. They were speaking in loud, pointed tones to me and for our generation.

I idolized these musicians and wanted to emulate them. I played guitar in a small band during my sophomore and junior years of high school, but I was only good on guitar, probably even less competent on vocals—and I lugged around a massive fear of singing and playing in front of people. The best I could do was fortify myself for each performance by getting high enough to escape my stage fright and sing the two or three songs on which I sang lead. My favorite was singing lead on The Beatles' "A Day in the Life," which we managed to perform respectably well just one week after the *Sgt. Pepper's Lonely Hearts Club Band* album came out.

I was, as the expression goes, dazed and confused. I was uncertain about who I was and had no idea of who I wanted to be. I floundered in school. I rarely took my books out of my locker. I preferred to sit numbly through my classes, waiting for the 11:15 a.m. bell to ring and release me to go to work. Each day I'd show up, sometimes high and always bored, only to sit in the back of the class barely paying attention to the classroom activity. During impromptu tests, I'd cheat off others sitting nearby. More often than not, I just guessed at the answers. In multiple-choice quizzes, sometimes it suited me to make the marks in the A, B, C, and D columns of the answer sheet into some symmetrical pattern, not caring what the real answer might be. Mostly, I spent my time in class daydreaming about work or what I would be doing that night.

In the spring of 1968, I barely graduated from high school. I was among the select group whose parents were sent notices in April indicating we wouldn't graduate in June if we didn't complete additional work. For me, that meant re-taking three tests I'd previously failed and reading three books and writing book reports on them. I barely got the job done, and I confess that I cheated on half of it. I remember my dad pulling me aside one evening shortly after receiving the notice and saying, "I don't care how you do it, just do whatever it takes to graduate." That is what I did.

The Monday after graduation I went to work full-time, and longtime friend depression started rolling through me. Here I was, a barely-graduated, 17-year-old kid with a jail sentence for a job, lost and wondering what to do with my life. I didn't consider college because my grades were mostly D's sprinkled with some F's and an occasional C. My feeling about school to that point was that it had been a total waste of time and energy.

One day while I was eating lunch after laying down some lovely welding beads on a large aqueduct gate, I overheard a couple of co-workers talking about their experience in the Army and Vietnam. Their conversation got me thinking about my friend Brad D., who had just finished artillery school at Fort Sill, Oklahoma and was headed off to Vietnam. Brad was a creative guy, a year older than me. He also had a wild streak to go with his hot pale yellow, 1967 SS-396 Chevy Chevelle. Brad's Army stories and now the stories of these two other guys stuck in my mind. I don't know whether I was romanticizing the Army or whether I was just sick and tired of sweating under the welding helmet and hating my life. But an idea was germinating. To be clear, I was still firmly ensconced in the life laid out by Choice Three. Work and earn. Simple preservation. Being a good son in the eyes of my parents, the other two paths, at least for now, were ruled out.

Then, driving home one day near my 18th birthday in July of 1968, I saw an Army recruiting office. I stopped and went in to get some information about what the Army offered. When I walked out, I had signed up with a 60-day deferred entry date: Monday, September 23, 1968.

That evening, as my mother served us one of her delicious impromptu meals, I decided to tell my parents right there at the dinner table what I had done. They were shocked. I could feel the air being sucked out of the room as I laid out my plans. They had lots of questions and fears about my going to Vietnam and getting shot. I had given little thought to the possibility that I might die in Vietnam. Was that ignorance? Or my youthful belief that I was invincible? Whatever, I didn't care about my life and didn't feel it was worth much.

Before the tribunal of my parents, my failures had become the elephant in the room that I could no longer ignore. What had I done with my life so far? Get high on drugs and alcohol, have meaningless or failed relationships with girls, fail at school, and work at pointless jobs. If I ran away to San Francisco to become a full-time hippie, or if I ran away to India to follow a yogi or even become one, I would disappoint my family.

I recalled a failed attempt at running away earlier in the year. I'd gotten into another argument with my parents about my grades at school, how I was living my life, and what I was planning on doing with it. So, I took off suddenly late in the evening. I didn't have much cash for food and gas and only had the clothes on my back. I'd have to go to the bank the next day to get money to go somewhere. To get through the night, I ended up going to Kona Lanes, a bowling alley that was open 24 hours a day. I hunkered down on one of the booths at the end of a lane and started to sleep. I was abruptly awakened by a Costa Mesa police sergeant named George Alexander. We knew each other well because he had been my baseball coach for three years in the City's youth's baseball league. I liked him a lot. He asked me what I was doing, and after I told him, he urged me to head home on my own accord or else he'd have to call my parents, and they'd have to pick me up at the station. I headed back. I'm not sure my parents even knew I had run away.

One pattern of behavior that I had noticed myself embrace over the past few years was ignoring my unhappiness until I could no longer tolerate it. Then, to release the pain, I would merely make a radical move to shake things up. I did this with girlfriends, friends, drugs, work, and school. Of course, the one component of my life that I couldn't change was my parents. My strategy for dealing with them had always been merely to hide from them.

My parents, therefore, knew little about what was going on within me, so it was no wonder they couldn't understand why I would do something as out of the blue as signing up for the Army. I didn't understand my decision either. I did know, being disenchanted with everything, I was questioning the worth of my life and of life itself.

For months before I enlisted, my questions about life flowed inside me like a large spigot of water pouring into an 8-ounce cup, and the overflow had now become overwhelming and constant. The liquid was running everywhere, and everything was getting soaked. Nothing could contain all my questions, and I had no answers. I was drowning.

I had tried to find answers that fitted to the standard of my working-middle-class life. I attempted religion, as fashion, by speaking with numerous religious people, including the founders of The Calvary Chapel in Costa Mesa/Santa Ana, California, and by attending lots of different church services. Religion seemed wrong for me because it is filled with more rules, regulations, and unsubstantiated beliefs, which my intuition told me were possibly incorrect, not credible, and mostly not believable. Most religions appeared to be based on fear, and I couldn't see how any of them would help me understand my life's truth.

Drugs, especially pot and bennies, and alcohol offered me ways to dilute my pain, suffering, and sorrow. LSD was especially liberating. I took it for the first time with my friend Randy and immediately it expanded my mind in an odd and unusual way. Randy and I were motorcycle friends. He and I used to work on and ride our motorcycles together everywhere. Although he was shorter than me, he was bold and adventurous, a buddy who was always up for experimenting with booze, drugs, and life.

I'll never forget my first LSD trip one winter's night around 9:00 p.m. The night sky was dark and vibrant. Randy and I had gone to a rocky beach near the southern border of the exclusive beach town Corona Del Mar and its southern neighbor Laguna Beach. We parked along Pacific Coast Highway and walked down

Cameo Shores Road to the ocean, down a short stairway to the small beach. Crossing the sand, we headed north toward the rocky tidal area of the coast. Climbing around the rock bend, we ended up in a quiet, secluded cove.

Dropping our tabs of "Blue Owsley," we didn't talk much while we waited and watched the ocean roll in and out through the natural rock channels. Nothing seemed to be happening. Then, looking up, I saw a bright blue flash cut across the ocean's horizon. Looking for Randy to ask if he'd seen the same thing, I didn't see him.

At first, his absence didn't freak me out, but it did unnerve me. Even so, I was overcome by the sparkling stars, which were almost like tiny camera bulb flashes in the sky, bright, glittery, and intense. Looking down from where I was standing, I saw the jagged rocks as sharp and clean and holding their own as the ocean pounded relentlessly against them.

But paranoia and fear were slowly creeping up. Turning every which way to locate my friend and guide for my first psychedelic trip, I didn't see Randy. Now the ocean seemed to be getting angry, coming after me. The water charged up the rock channels toward me as though the angry, foam-headed waves wanted to eat me. Backing up to escape the hungry water monster, I bumped into the rock cliff. I thought this is it. In my panic and at the top of my lungs, I yelled, "Randy!", and he popped out from behind a rock where he had been sitting and said, "Huh?"

In an instant, my fear and paranoia fell away, and all was right with the world. The outstanding thing after those moments of abject terror was how everything seemed clear, sharp, and crisp. I felt that I saw reality—all of existence—far more clearly than I'd ever seen it before. Whether I saw truth, I don't know, but I do know that I felt a rightness in all that I sensed and saw. It was as though I'd stepped into a different dimension.

Many of my LSD trips did have their pitfalls. One time I was driving down the street and all the dashed white lines between lanes became solid cement like pillars extending to the sky. Because I couldn't see the cars traveling in adjacent lanes, it was impossible to change lanes safely until the intersections, which was not only dangerous but also illegal.

I had hoped that LSD and the other drugs I was taking would change the "me" that I was into some ideal version of me. To a minor extent, the drug seemed to be changing me in some way, but not with the results I had hoped for and certainly not fast enough. In the end, the drugs and booze only seemed to dull the throb of sadness, and I kept waking up to the same person I was before. I didn't want to keep relying on LSD as if it were a magic potion. Just like when the Army offered me a way to change my life quickly, I simply said "yes."

That is how I often made decisions. It was as if I would drive down the same street for some time and then have a clear realization that the road was going nowhere, or nowhere I wanted to go. So, at the next corner, I would turn and take a new direction. I was a living embodiment of the remark often attributed, but unfounded, to Albert Einstein, "The definition of insanity is doing the same thing over and over again and expecting a different result." My habit of changing directions to escape from myself had me doing pretty much just that. I didn't realize until much later that my problem wasn't the path that I was on. My issue was my sense of who I was.

Although most of my turns in direction lacked much forethought, each new course did inch me forward toward self-awareness, and signing my life away for three years of active duty certainly set me up for a truckload of hard life lessons.

At the reinstitution and drawing of the Selective Service Draft, my birthdate was number 67 in the lottery and that the first 195 numbers would be called up to serve. Being 67, plus my not having a 2-S student education deferment, meant that I would have been drafted anyway. There was no way around it: I didn't have fervent enough anti-war beliefs to go to Canada or jail. I was going into the Army, no matter what.

As my chosen induction day got closer, I quit work, hung out with friends, took a couple of trips to San Francisco, went to the beach and body-surfed, and waited to take on my new adventure.

I knew I wasn't a Dr. Timothy Leary's "turn on, tune in, drop out" type of guy anyway. Yes, my personal beliefs about war, our "great society," and how life is supposed to work were camped in the peace and love movement; however, I was raised to conform to the standards set by my parents and my forefathers. I felt an unstated pressure to conform to society regardless of my personal beliefs and to believe that our country's leaders knew what they were doing.

Both my parents came from families that had strong religious beliefs and that people described as "salt of the earth." We were working stock, and we followed the rules. We trusted our government and probably lived by the motto "In God We Trust," although in our house we rarely, talked about God, religion, or ever went to church.

My brother and I were raised, much like my parents were, with the fear of being punished for our wrongdoings or for breaking society's rules. The spare the rod, spoil the child philosophy lived in our home. This saying coming from Proverbs 13:24 that, the New American Standard Bible, states; "He who withholds his rod hates his son, But he who loves him disciplines him diligently." Neither parent held back physical punishment based on their rules of how my brother and I needed to act.

My mother's Catholic family immigrated from France, via Quebec, and ended up working in the woolen mills of Northbridge, Massachusetts. Everyone in her family and just about everyone in town worked in these mills. My great aunt, at 80 years old, ran a specialized type of loom, locked in a special room so that government inspectors wouldn't find her. She was well past legal working age, and she was one of the few remaining people who knew the details of how that complex loom worked.

My dad's Lutheran family, whose roots were in England, Germany, Ireland, and Norway, lived in Mobridge, a small town on the plains of South Dakota. His father was a railroad worker and line inspector who was gone most of the time. His mother was a general-store merchant. She worked long, hard hours alone while her husband was away. They never had much, but they always got by. As an only child, my dad spent a lot of his growing-up time alone, but he and his best friend, Keith Denzen, enjoyed building forts and going on made-up adventures on the banks of the Missouri River. He told me how cold and harsh the winters were, and he wondered how the "Indians" in the nearby Standing Rock Reservation made it through each one in "tents."

For me to go against our family tradition of hard work without a strong sense of self and confidence was almost unthinkable. So, I did what came to me in my own mixed up way. I participated in the hippie revolution at the level I could get away with, without being thrown in jail, and I engaged with various parts of the new order when it seemed safe enough to do so. I took care of my personal and financial needs, but now a deeper calling, one that was questioning my place in the world, was propelling me in a new direction. It was leading me away from this family tradition of merely working, but I didn't know how to reach out to it. I felt adrift in the sea of life without paddles, compass, or map.

Lastly, my decision to join the Army was influenced by my dad's company having a very rough time of it. As one would expect from a dedicated family man, he did what he had to do to earn extra money and keep food on the table, which included delivering the *Los Angeles Times* newspaper at 3:00 a.m. every morning to residences in Lido Island, Linda Island, Balboa Island and the Balboa Peninsula, some of the most exclusive neighborhoods in Orange County. I knew his commitment to his family and that he would do this until he was financially back on his feet. Wanting to be helpful and supportive of the family, I loaned my dad money. What's more, I sensed my struggles, moodiness, and lack of direction wasn't making life any more comfortable in the house. Therefore, leaving home seemed like the best thing to do.

Chapter 5

We're in The Army Now

On September 23, 1968, I boarded a bus in Los Angeles and headed to Monterey, California to begin my career as a soldier.

A high level of anticipatory energy created by the recruits filled the bus on the long ride from the L.A. Army Recruitment Center to Fort Ord. We were a motley crew in those 20 rows of seats; friends murmuring, while others sat alone gazing out of the windows at the passing scenery with dazed, lost-in-thought looks in their eyes. Still, others were making new friends, something I learned happens quickly in the Army.

Just south of Santa Barbara, I struck up a conversation with my seatmate, a tall, thin African American who was smoking Kool cigarettes. He offered me one, and we discussed the satisfaction and rewards of our particular cigarette brand preferences. Two Hawaiians sitting directly in front of us overheard our conversation, quickly turned around and jumped on my new friend's Kool bandwagon while I was the lone

Marlboro defender. We laughed to ease our tensions about our destination and any trepidation around our cultural and racial differences melted away like butter on a hot pancake.

Just outside of Buellton (Home of "Pea Soup Anderson's"), my seatmate, James, told me his story. He had never met his dad. He was brought up in a single-parent home with a revolving door of "uncles." James had gotten into several fights while growing up. Some of the fights were in response to what people said about his mom; others were in defense of his manhood when other boys tried to make a mark for themselves through violence. "Man, I hate to fight jackasses who think they're better 'n me," he told me as the bus rolled into the late evening.

As the light of the day disappeared and the dark of the night crept into the bus, he talked about how he had disliked everything about school, the regimen, the seeming uselessness of it. He said, "What was I gonna learn that was gonna make my life better?" He had missed so much school growing up that he was a couple of years behind others his age. He felt misplaced and stupid because all the kids in his classes were younger and looked down at him. Like me, he had barely graduated. Once they pushed him out of high school he was unable to find work and was feeling a lot of pressure to "bring somethin' home; you know what I mean?" Part of the problem of getting work was that he had spent time in juvie for stealing, and employers didn't want to give him a chance "cause I had a rap sheet," he stated. During the early summer of 1968, he got caught stealing again, and this time the judge gave him a choice, "Go into the Army or go to jail." And probably, like at least half of us on this bus, he chose the Army because he didn't know what else to do, and for him, the Army sounded better than jail.

This bus was full of misfits, clinging together as people do when faced with a shared unknown and heading for a life-changing event. Being from different socioeconomic, racial, and cultural backgrounds made no difference as we were just a bus full of guys anxiously wondering what was next. For each of us, there was a scared or unsure child inside being touched by the vast unknown. Some were being moved more than others as our behavior ran the gamut from bravado to stillness. All of us knew we had no idea what was going to happen next.

We arrived at Fort Ord around 2:00 a.m., which made for an exciting introduction. We were herded off the bus, told to stand in straight rows and to line up behind the guy in front of us. Standing there in the cold, foggy Coastal California night, I shook from both the chill of the air and because men with "Smokey the Bear" hats with raised, intense voices told us what to do and what we should know. I tuned out on most of it but remember one distinct thing: "…You'll get a break from us tomorrow morning because you won't have to get up until 7:00 a.m. And at 8:00 a.m. Sergeant Montoya will march you to chow."

Indeed, promptly at 8:00 a.m., a wide-eyed, short-statured sergeant in a starched-and-creased uniform with a raging voice, paced us through fast and furious activity including breakfast which was followed by filling out a bunch of forms. Then we took aptitude tests, got haircuts and uniforms, and moved into our barracks, home for the next couple of months. After we found our bunks, instructions on how to make a bed, pack a footlocker, how to dress, and how to address each other. After lunch, the lessons continued with how to salute, march, eat and obey anyone who had stripes, bars, clusters, and stars. If we said "Yes Sir!" to a non-officer, a drill instructor (DI) would scream, "I work for a living; it's 'Yes Sergeant!'"

All this information shared with us through yelling, intimidation and demeaning commands. It was nothing for a DI to pick someone out in the group, stand about six inches away from the soldier, and bark at him in a way that would put fear in him. By intimidating one of us, they aimed to scare all of us into following their growled instructions without question.

The first subject of the DI's wrath was Clark. Clark seemed like an easygoing, slightly heavy guy that may not have seemed smart on the outside, but I sensed he was knowledgeable. His downfall, for the sergeants, was that he had no rhythm. Every time we marched in cadence or double-timed somewhere, Clark was immediately out of step. After yelling at him for days, they finally realized that wasn't going to work, so they put him in the very back of each marching formation so that he wouldn't screw up the others trying to march in cadence. But the yelling continued, and I could see him trying to keep rhythm but failing within 5 to 10 steps, causing the screaming to start all over again. It felt as if the sergeants had no compassion or understanding of what it might be like to be Clark, a man with no natural rhythm.

By the end of the third day of my soldiering experience, I decided that I had made an error by joining the Army. After giving some thought to my predicament, I determined that my best course of action was to ask one of the sergeants if I could get out of my commitment. The next day, when there was a brief lull in our activities after midday chow, I walked up to Sergeant Montoya and asked if there was a way I could change my mind about my enlistment.

Immediately, I could tell I had said the wrong thing. Montoya's anger quickly rose to the surface, and as his face contorted, he became unglued, hurling nasty insults I'd never heard before. He acted as if I had killed his entire family! With spit flying out of his mouth and landing all over my face, he told me, "Your sorry-ass life is mine. And being that you're from California, you're either a queer or dog shit, and you don't look or smell like dog shit to me."

Ordering me to the ground, he yelled "Give me a hundred," so I dutifully, laboriously, and painfully did one hundred pushups. While I was pushing myself away from the ground, he informed me that he would be watching my every move because now he knew I was a "fuckup and troublemaker." I was now on his shit list, just like Clark, but differently.

That day, I learned that some decisions in life are meant to be ridden out without attempting to change them. This decision being one of them, I was hopeful I'd learned a valuable lesson.

My response to landing on Montoya's shit list was to lie low. However, my success at doing that lasted only a couple of weeks, until my group was sent to get another haircut and I decided that I didn't need one. While being herded through the barbershop, I walked in the front door, went straight through the shop and out the back door, and returned to the barracks.

At chow that cold, rainy evening, one of the other sergeants came up to me and shouted, "Did you go to the barbershop with the rest of the troops?"

"Yes, Sergeant," I said. I was truthful to his question. I had gone to the barbershop. I just hadn't stopped to get a haircut.

He smacked me in the back of the head and yelled, "UP!" With the rest of the men in the chow hall watching intensely, he ordered me outside and told me to stand in the rain. After enduring the wet for about half an hour, another sergeant came up to me. "Low crawl around the barracks," he said. Low crawling is lying on your belly and moving your arms and legs in a crab-like manner, so you scoot along the ground.

"Yell out, 'I am a big-ass lying worm,'" he yelled at me, "so the people on the third floor can hear you." Dutifully I followed his orders for about three hours in the cold rain, which had turned the sparsely covered lawn into a mud pool. So much for lying low.

After Basic Training, my assignment was to Artillery Training School at Fort Sill, Oklahoma, for 16 weeks of AIT (Advanced Individual Training). Then, because of my test scores during Basic Training, my AIT was to be followed by NCOS (Non-Commissioned Officers School), also at Fort Sill.

I was initially asked to go to Officer Candidate School and declined, as it would have meant staying in the Army longer. At NCOS in Oklahoma, I would be trained as a sergeant and section chief for an artillery unit in Vietnam. Because this position was a quick way to move up in the ranks, people in the Army called us "Shake and Bake Sergeants." I also liked the idea of making more money while serving in the Army.

My time at Fort Sill was stressful, mainly because I was attempting to become an authority figure, as an artillery section chief, in a system I thoroughly despised. I was learning to lead soldiers with authority, call cadence as we marched across parade grounds, and guide a crew of men to fire all types of Army weaponry. All of this conflicted with my moral compass.

I began distancing myself from these duties by reviving the meditation practice that I had learned at the love-in at Irvine Park. Late at night as most everyone else was bunked down for the night, I would sit cross-legged on my bed and meditate to calm down and find peace. To set the tone, I would light a candle, then breathe gently in and out, tuning out the noise of everyone else's talk.

Each of us shared a low-walled living space with one other person. I was fortunate to share my space with Robert Cuddy who was from Connecticut. Mostly I was laughed at as a weirdo from California, but Cuddy was cool. Our brief conversations told me we were on the same wavelength and that he respected my meditation practice.

My time in Oklahoma wasn't all bad. For $100, I bought a 1959 two-toned Buick Electra that had a light seafoam green body and white top. I bought the car from a recent NCOS graduate who came from Kentucky and now headed to Vietnam. The two-speed Dynaflow automatic transmission was made for cruising the highways between Fort Sill and Oklahoma City or to Wichita Falls, Texas, for a day of exploration. Having a car and driving away from the base let me feel as if being in the Army was more of a job than a life.

I was also able to have a little fun while at Ft. Sill learning my job. Driving self-propelled howitzers (SPs) through the mud was exciting. An SP was like a tank but with a larger gun. We would propel the SP from one location to another, stop, set up, and shoot at targets that could be as much as a mile away. Again, being in control of a vehicle is what pleased me the most. I also came to enjoy learning how to march people in cadence. We used songs as a way of keeping people in step together. Instead of using typical Army marching songs, I adapted The Beatles' "Yellow Submarine" to march my troops. As the song, written in march time, was perfect: It allowed me to have fun, make fun of the Army, and show my individuality.

Upon completing my NCOS training, I got my orders to report for duty in Vietnam. Selling the Buick for $100 to another NCOS candidate, I headed home for a short leave before turning up at Alameda Naval Air Station on San Francisco Bay. In August of 1969, I boarded a flight to "the Nam."

The Apollo astronauts had just walked on the moon.

Chapter 6

Nam and Numb

"Look at all the fireworks in the air," the flight attendant said as we approached Vietnam's coastline.

We looked out the windows, our anxiety palpable beneath nervous murmurs of discussion that broke the tense quiet of the cabin. In the distance, we could see flaming red and white flares hanging in the sky. Looking towards the ground, we could see small groupings of lights that outlined small villages. Off the left side windows, toward the horizon, the burning street and house lights of Saigon loomed. My stomach was slowly twisting itself into deep knots at the thought that those flares, and the feelings they brought up, would be there for a long time.

"Oh my God," I thought, "what have I gotten myself into?" My situation felt very real, and it was about to get even more real.

Before I had time to let these new thoughts sink in, the intense silence was broken by a terse announcement, "Take your seats and buckle up for a hard and fast landing at Tan Son Nhut air base, Vietnam."

As soon as our wheels touched the ground, the roar of the reverse thrusters threw me against my seat belt, and hard, heavy braking brought our aircraft to a wildly screeching halt. After about a minute, the front door opened, and an Army staff sergeant bounded on board.

"Get off this plane NOW," he shouted. "The Viet Cong are welcoming you by trying to blow this sucker up. I want you to get your asses up out of your seats, head to either the front or rear exit, climb down the stairs, and throw yourselves into the ditch next to the runway. We'll let you know when it's time to get out of the ditch."

I'd never seen an evacuation of a plane before, so I have no comparison, but I can say we were off that plane pretty damn fast. The next thing I knew I was lying in the ditch next to the runway. The plane's lights were off, and it became spooky quickly in the warm, musty, moonless night. In the distance, we heard occasional explosions: mortars. As I lay there in the humid, dark night, I felt a growing awareness that my circumstances were not a surreal scene from some movie. They were real.

Lifting my head over the top of the ditch, all I could see was an expanse of flat ground ahead of me. The outline of the plane looked ghostly where it stood on the asphalt runway. To my left, the land was merely flat, dark and open. To my right was the outline of a set of buildings with lights off. Lying there, I wondered if the enemy was going to come running up and simply shoot me there in the ditch.

The next day I discovered that the air base we had landed on was a vast complex run by the Army and that there had been no danger of being shot by a rifle. Our only real immediate threat at that time was being mortared or rocketed, still, a threat that was very real.

My assignment to Bravo Battery of the 1st Battalion, 7th Field Artillery, in the 1st Infantry Division ("Big Red One") took just a couple of days. I would be taking the place of a sergeant as section chief on a 105 mm howitzer. Within two days I was sitting in the back of a supply deuce and a half (2½ ton truck) on my way to my unit. At a lunch stop, I heard that Baltag, a friend of mine from basic and artillery training in Oklahoma, had been killed by a landmine along with some others as they traveled in a convoy heading north. It wasn't easy to hop back on the truck, but what were my options? There was a lot of open space and jungle out there and going AWOL didn't seem like a real choice.

During the second night with my new artillery unit, I was in our underground bunker attempting to get some sleep before our midnight fire mission. Suddenly, the current sergeant section chief, the one I'd be replacing, came flying down the crude ammo box-built stairs into our dug-out dirt-walled sleeping quarters with a wild gleam in his eyes. "Grab your guns!" he shouted. "We got gooks on the wire." An enemy ground unit was attacking us, and they were at our barbed wire perimeter.

I grabbed my rifle and headed up top to see what to do. Our sergeant, who we did call "Sarge," caught my arm and pulled me as he ran toward the wire. Crouched behind a small stand of sandbags with the higher wall of sandbags protecting our howitzer behind me, I saw the barbed wire perimeter about 50 feet in front of me and started looking for people to shoot. Then, suddenly, a head popped up. I saw the flash from the muzzle of his rifle, heard a pop, and felt a small explosion as his bullet entered the sandbag next to my left shoulder. I immediately lifted my M-16 rifle, fired, and watched him fall backward.

A very odd rush of adrenaline, fear, and clarity ran through my body. At that moment, everything became unreal and real at the same time. The surreal night continued to unfold in a mix of looking, shooting, waiting, looking, shooting, wondering, and noise, lots of noise.

After about 45 minutes the small caliber fire ceased, but flares continued to float down from the sky from mortars and from a "Puff" that lit the area with a yellow glow. Puff was an AC-47 airplane that would fly in slow and steady circles around a firefight. Its mini Gatling guns fired 2,000 to 6,000 rounds a minute while it dropped flares that would hang in the air for 10 minutes or more, lighting up the ground below. The parachutes on these flares were at least eight feet across and seemed to hang forever while providing an ethereal light to fight.

Additionally, both sides used tracer bullets to assist the shooters' aim. The Viet Cong primarily used AK 47's with greenish tracers, while all U.S. tracers were a blazing red. A nighttime fight rivaled any light show put on by the Jefferson Airplane or The Grateful Dead, especially when Puff let loose its red tracer bullet streams from the sky. With every sixth bullet a tracer—sometimes every second or third—at 6,000 rounds per minute a lot of red poured out of Puff.

Those solid, thin red lines and the red and white flares hanging in the sky joined a cacophony of greenish and red tracers from rifles, yellowish bomb and mortar explosions, and flashes from other artillery explosions. Some of the exploding shells were packed with white phosphorus that produced a greenish-white glow while it burned. All of this created quite a show that one could sit back and stare at in awe and wonder if one were not dodging bullets.

Early the next morning after our firefight and our artillery mission, which lasted until 4:00 a.m., we were summoned by our battery captain and told we had to go out, count, and then neatly stack enemy bodies as one would stack cordwood. Counting bodies were part of the reporting cycle our government used to demonstrate to the public that we were winning the war. By reporting the enemy "body count" compared with the U.S. "body count," the newspapers back home could spin the story.

As we counted and stacked bodies, my curiosity led me to the area where I had shot my first bullet at a human being. It didn't take me long to find the body. He had yet to be stacked. He was lying right where knew I'd see him. Turning back toward my gun position, I immediately validated that he was the one. I felt myself go numb. "I killed somebody." Hiding my tears and sadness from the other men, I wondered what I was doing here and how I could kill another human being. I felt as though someone had hit me hard across the face. My jaw dropped, and I felt myself slip into a state close to shock.

Then my feelings turned to anger and disgust as I watched other GIs having their pictures taken with their feet on the chests or heads of our fallen enemy in a show of courage, strength, and triumph. Some were leaning up against the stacked bodies in poses of bravery and achievement as if they were proud of killing.

Turning back to the dead body lying at my feet; I realized he was somebody's son, and maybe a brother, uncle, dad, nephew, and friend. He was just like me, but he was dead, and I was alive. How was God going to forgive me for doing this? How was I ever going to forgive myself?

Sadness, like a slow-moving tsunami ingesting a shoreline, enveloped me. I could feel everything closing in on me from the inside out. The tears blurring out my outward vision enhanced my stark realization that I'd lost clarity. I was numb.

Despite my history of telling lies, cheating, and other indiscretions, today felt like I had lost my human innocence. I was now a killer and my humanness, compromised.

The sergeant I was replacing was leaving in a week, and all day long he kept telling me how great it was that he could "kill some more gooks" before he left. What a contrast to my experience. All I could think was, "God, how did I get here and how do I get through this?" Even worse, "Would I end up like him and like killing?"

During my first seven months in Vietnam, the section under my command was involved in only about a half-dozen direct, face to face, encounters like that one. Each time we had a firefight, though, it felt surreal to me. Most of my participation in the war, outside of these few direct firefights, was indirect but with even more devastating results. Our battery of six 105 mm howitzers moved every two to four weeks to some remote place, usually a meadow or clearing surrounded by jungle or rice paddies. We would dig in, create some temporary sandbag shelters for ourselves and our artillery shells, and begin supporting infantry units doing "search and destroy" missions in the jungle. Often the fighting was close enough for us to see the explosions our rounds were making. If it was within a click (1,000 meters), we could be asked to venture outside of our little circle of guns and take body counts to verify the kills. Fortunately, in most of these firefights, we were not directly attacked except by mortars.

One of the scariest experiences any artillery battery can have is to watch enemy mortar rounds walk up a meadow toward its position. On occasions when this would happen, we would take cover until we'd get the battle cry, "BATTERY ADJUST," which meant that we were about to engage the enemy with our howitzers. This was followed by very specific instructions through our radios from the Fire Direction Center (FDC) on how to aim our howitzer by a particular deflection or azimuth (left and right angle of the barrel), quadrant or elevation (up and down angle of the barrel), and charge (amount of gunpowder charge in the shell). A set of aiming stakes determined deflection we laid out and calibrated when we set up in a new area and recalibrated each morning. Once our gun was ready, we'd inform the battery commander. We had to respond quickly because a mortar round hitting our ammunition could cause devastating damage to life and equipment.

The sequence from the FDC went like this: "BATTERY ADJUST, deflection 314, quadrant 24.5, charge 3." I would repeat the instructions, loudly, to my gun crew. The assistant gunner would shout the deflection, the gunner would shout out the elevation, and the primary loader would state the charge. When the crew members validated their assignments and had them ready, they would shout "Ready," and I would shout "Number 4 is ready" and raise my right-hand high. At night, we had a red-lensed flashlight that we'd point at the FDC when our gun was ready.

We practiced getting ready often because our lives and the lives of soldiers we were supporting depended on our doing it quickly and accurately. Even if we were sleeping, we could be up and ready to fire at specific enemy positions in under 70 seconds. At night, it could take a few seconds longer to find and align our sights on our red- and green-lit aiming posts, but efficient speed was the order of the day, every day.

Did I ever screw up? Yes. After spending three nights in a row firing thousands of rounds near Cu Chi trying to destroy the Viet Cong's tunnels, we had a night of respite. However, an assault on a platoon of U.S. GIs required us to man our guns and support them with a fire mission. The cry "BATTERY ADJUST" rang out and we were at our guns again. After repeating the fire instructions to my crew, we swung into action moving the gun around, loaded the chamber with a charge 5 round and I shouted: "number 4 is ready!" The fire chief shouted "battery fire," and all six howitzers fired their rounds.

What I noticed right away was that my gun's muzzle flash was almost in the exact opposite direction from the other gun's flashes. FDC relayed new adjustment commands, and over the radio, I told FDC and the fire chief "number 4 is out." Being out, meant I wouldn't be able to continue the fire mission as there was something wrong with my gun. I told my crew to stand down and not to touch anything. My deepest fear was that we fired an explosive round and had no idea where it landed. Did it hit US soldiers, a village, a city, the enemy, or in the middle of the jungle? Regardless only FDC would be able to calculate where this round had landed.

After the mission completed, the officer in charge of FDC and his staff sergeant came over and started investigating what happened. As I told them, my gunner had aligned on the wrong set of aiming posts, and I didn't validate his work. Using some simple geometry, we figured out my gun's deflection by noting the aiming posts he used. Then with the stated quadrant and charge, the FDC staff could calculate where my round landed—in a rice patty.

It was a scary and sad moment. Although the outcome was good, all I could think about is how easy it was to screw up and kill someone unintentionally.

During rare moments when attacked on our perimeter, we would lower the gun barrels to horizontal and shoot with fuses set on muzzle action so that the round would explode a few feet upon leaving the barrel. The types of shells fused for this sort of event were white phosphorous and beehive.

With white phosphorous or "Willy Peter" as we called it, the muzzle blast would spread burning phosphorous toward the intended target. The most horrible thing about Willy Peter was that it burned through the skin until no more oxygen got to it. Hearing people scream out because of the pain of WP burning through their bodies was crazy-making. Sometimes the screaming would last a half hour or more, and at night this sound would be haunting.

The other round, the beehive, was horrible in a much different way. Inside this round were 8,000 tiny nail-like darts (flechettes), sharp on one end with fins on the other. The muzzle blast and the shaped charge in the shell would propel the darts with high speed into their intended targets. So powerful were these blasts that when doing our body counts, I found people nailed to trees and their rifles nailed to them.

We were not always fighting. Sometimes nothing would happen for a day or two, and we'd sit in the humid jungle heat or wet monsoon cleaning ourselves or our guns. Then suddenly, we'd hear "BATTERY ADJUST," which usually meant that an infantry group was either being attacked or had stumbled on an enemy position and wanted to surprise them with artillery.

After seven months of the constant teeter-totter of life and death, the Army announced on the Armed Forces Radio Network that the Big Red One was going home. What that meant for most of us who had been in the 1st Infantry Division was reassignment to other units in Vietnam. I found out I was assigned to the 3rd Battalion, 11th Field Artillery of the 101st Airborne Division (the famous "Screaming Eagles") in the most northern part of South Vietnam next to the Demilitarized Zone (DMZ). They also offered me the choice of taking the "early out" program. This option entailed staying in Vietnam for more than my current overseas obligation of one year. If I stayed until I had five months remaining in my total three-year active duty Army obligation, then I could leave Vietnam, return stateside, and be discharged without serving the last five months of my enlistment. As an added incentive, I could take an extra 30-day leave.

It didn't take me long to decide that I wanted out of the Army more than I was afraid of dying in Vietnam, so I took advantage of the program. Did I spend any time thinking about this decision? Probably not. Whether from bravado, the stupidity of youth, or knowing somehow after my first firefight that I wouldn't die in Vietnam, I decided to stay. What I knew was that I hated the Army more and therefore I wanted out as soon as I could.

I took my 30-day leave stateside and returned to Vietnam in March of 1970. When I arrived back in Vietnam, I got in a jeep and driven to Phu Bai, my new post. My new commanders quickly noticed that I didn't hear them very well during conversations. They ordered hearing tests that determined that I would be a liability in charge of a 155 mm howitzer, a bigger gun than my previous 105 mm. They were concerned that I wouldn't hear crucial commands and that the louder sounds and concussion from the larger guns would add to my growing hearing deficit.

To make use of me, they assigned me to a Military Assistance Command–Vietnam (MACV) unit in the city of Hue, the ancient imperial capital of Vietnam made famous in the United States because of the 1968 Tet Offensive.

My job, in this liaison position, was to clear (approve) areas for air strikes by B-52 bombers, Air Force fighter jets, and the U.S. Navy, which was shooting 8 and 16-inch cannons from ships stationed off the coast. Although the fighter attacks and navel artillery were rarer, the B-52 strikes were a regular occurrence. I worked under a captain and had two specialists working for me. The captain rarely came to our well-fortified underground bunker under one of the ancient citadel buildings in central Hue. The walls of the bunkered rooms in which we worked were lined almost floor to ceiling with maps. On these maps, we placed pins noting the currently known locations of all US Army personnel, the 1ˢᵗ Arvin Division (Vietnamese Army) locations, and known friendly villages.

In another room down the hall, there was a U.S. Air Force command station with radios to communicate with the pilots of the planes scheduled to drop bombs on cleared targets. Adjacent to the Air Force office was an office for the Navy that coordinated the shelling of specific territory by their warships. Also, just a few short yards from our office was a "war room" that had a vast array of electronic equipment including a large grey box in the middle of the floor with a red phone on it. The war room always had at least two people manning the phones and radios. The red phone, I was told, was a direct line to the Pentagon war room.

Requests to bomb a specific area would come to us via radio, phone, or from the other men down the hall. We would review our latest intelligence and our maps on "friendly" locations, and if it looked OK, we would check in the next room that housed our Vietnamese counterparts, who would review the maps of their army divisions and provide approval or disapproval. Once approved, we would contact the bombing command and issue a "go order." All of this had a paper trail with required signoffs. On occasion, I would go out with my interpreter to view the bombing from a distance and sadness would overtake me as I felt the ground rumble from the hundreds of explosions that I knew were killing Viet Cong and maybe other innocent people. In viewing a bombed site, there were times when all you would find is crater after crater of smoldering dirt, water, rice, forest, and bodies.

After a few months of doing this job, I started realizing how many deaths I was participating in. Thousands of people were dying because we were approving air strikes in Vietnam, Cambodia, and Laos. The number of people dying in these strikes depressed me immensely and led me to find and use more drugs than I had already been using to numb my mind.

On occasion, my interpreter Huy N. and I would head out after a shift, and I would find myself in some fascinating places. Huy was a slight young man with a roundish head and piercing dark-brown eyes. He had lost his family while he was studying at a university in Saigon. It was there Huy learned English and decided to use his new language skills to help his country. His quick, easy smile was infectious, and he got along with everyone. In Vietnamese, the meaning of his name—bright light—reflected his spirit. He was adept at showing me some of the cultural sites and history of Hue. Through him, I was able to visit the tomb of Emperor Minh Mang (1820 – 1840 AD), and introduced to a family he knew that was hiding and protecting three solid gold Buddha statues from being captured by either side. I also visited Chua Thien Mu (Heavenly Lady Pagoda and temple) built in 1601 AD consisting of the Pagoda and a Buddhist temple where a few monks lived. The monk who so famously protested the dictatorship of South Vietnam's Ngo Dinh Diem's government by immolating himself on the street in Saigon came from this temple.

Huy also supplied me with my regular stash of pot, hash, and some of my other favorite drug choices. During one of our ventures outside the walls of the MACV compound, I found myself in a small dark room stuck in a middle of a maze of other places and buildings and off an alleyway that smelled of musky dirt and humidity. I was sitting there with a smiling old Vietnamese man and my interpreter and handed a pipe filled with an opium derivative of some sort. After taking a couple of huge hits, I was gone. My first thought after I realized I had merely fallen backward and into the wall behind me was, "Up against the wall, motherfuckers," recalling a line from a Jefferson Airplane song "We Can Be Together." The sensation was heavenly quiet, dead and alive at the same time.

My daily intake of drugs changed at that point. Initially, I was smoking some incredible Thai-stick weed and occasionally hash along with occasionally imported psychedelics from the States. I had now moved on to opium, and early in the last eight months of my stay in Vietnam, I tried heroin for the very first time. Although the heroin was 95%+ pure China White, I believed that by smoking it laced inside my Marlboro Cigarettes, I could have all the pleasures of the drug without getting hooked.

Buying the China White was easy. It came in small vials and could easily be carried anywhere. Occasionally, I'd buy it from Huy, but generally, I got it from fellow soldiers who had their supply chains. Lacing the substance into cigarettes was simple because you didn't need much to obtain the effect of being softly sealed off from the world. I'd take a cigarette, roll the end between my fingers to loosen up the tobacco and aim the open end toward a table top to catch the loosened tobacco. Opening the vial, I'd pour a small amount of the heroin into the open end and tap the filtered end of the cigarette on the table top to distribute the white powder through the pre-loosened tobacco. Putting some of remaining spilled tobacco back into the end, I'd refashion the cigarette almost to its original shape.

Lighting it up and taking a few drags would begin the sojourn into a numbed world where the tensions of killing people didn't exist.

As time floated by with this soft sponge around my head, I could complete my work, make time go by without much mental conflict, and make it to the next day with few side effects. I had friends with whom I got high, and sometimes we would play cards or jam on guitars till we slipped off into our own private sleepy, no worries, drug-and-alcohol-induced worlds.

I was soon to learn the painful truth about my drug use. About two months before I was to leave Vietnam for the second and final time, one of my drug buddies got his ticket to go home. In celebration of his making it through his tour, our group had a massive blow-out for his last night, ingesting all the drugs and booze we put on the table.

My buddy did not get off scot-free. About 12 hours after he left to catch his plane home, he called me in a panic from the airport at Cam Ranh Bay.

"I need you to bring me some stuff," he said. "I think I'm hooked. I need something NOW." He wanted me to get a jeep and drive miles across the war-torn countryside at night to take him some of our beloved China White. At first, I was flabbergasted. I didn't think he could be hooked. We had only smoked it. We weren't shooting it up.

"Come on," he pressed, "I need you to bring me some stuff." I told him I couldn't get a jeep, let alone drive out of our military compound without a permit to deliver drugs to him. Needless to say, when he realized I wasn't going to be able to drive over to help him, he got furious, called me an "asshole" and a "no-good motherfucker," and slammed down the phone.

The next morning, I reflected on our conversation and began to wonder if I was hooked. Suddenly, my mind went numb as a wave of realization crashed down through my body. It was the sort of recognition I would have had if my best friend had caught me stealing from him. I felt a flush of embarrassment mixed with sadness and fear. The realization scared me to the marrow of my bones. I was just six weeks short of finally heading home, and now I visualized myself going back hooked on heroin and landing in the street or locked away in a mental hospital just like my oldest cousin, who had also become addicted to heroin while in the service. My heartache and sadness for my cousin, his eventual drug-induced death, and the sorrow and pain it brought to his family, was enormous. My head became flushed with blood as the thoughts and consequences of not living up to my family's expectations, nor my expectations hit home.

I had been raised to do the right thing, to work long and hard at any job I had, like my father and his father. There were times my dad would work 12 hours a day, seven days a week, to ensure food on the table and a roof over our heads. He was my model. I learned that my actions represented our family and me in the world. I was raised to be proud of my work and accomplishments. My family always looked good when one looked at us from the outside, regardless of any difficulty there may have been going on within it. Hooked on heroin would be very detrimental, at the very least, to how our family would be perceived, and I didn't want to be the cause of any negative perceptions.

On top of this worry was the concern for my safety. I'd seen hooked needle users succumb to their addiction. I'd witnessed their drug overdoses, and I'd watched the demise of their lives. I did not want to choose the life of the setting sun, as it was called, never to see it rise again. I resolved to find out if I was hooked and if so, to get clean as soon as possible.

It was in mid-to-late March 1971. Because I was due time off and had already trained my replacement, it was the perfect time to just stop my use of the drug and see what happened. My seniority and my time in the country (nearly 19 months at this juncture) had earned me my own small room in the northwest edge of a building that was itself located on the northwest edge of the MACV compound. It was as far as possible from the prying eyes of the officer billets, about as isolated as you could get on this small military complex in the middle of downtown Hue. I asked my closest friends for assistance, telling them to check in on me from time to time, drop off water and some food, and be willing to sit with me if they saw that I needed it. And I made them all promise not to give me any drugs, no matter what I said or pleaded. I met with my commanding officer and told the captain that I would be unavailable during my last few weeks in-country as I had some personal business to resolve.

"I don't have a problem with that," he said. "You've done a good job for me, and giving you extra time off would be my pleasure."

I stocked up on some necessary items including food, cigarettes, chocolate, and lots of water in spare canteens. I told Monky, a tiny, old Vietnamese woman who did my laundry, made my bed and kept my room spotless, that I wouldn't need her to clean up my room for a couple of weeks and that she would not need to come by my hooch. I didn't need her prying eyes or any gossip among the local Vietnamese help who worked inside the compound. Closing the door, looking around the room, the thought of holing up for a week or two seemed oddly scary and inviting. As I lay on my bed that night, I wondered what was going to happen to me.

When my life requires it, I do have a powerful will, and for the next couple of weeks, I 'd be tested. I was stepping off into the unknown. I had made the decision and was clear about what I wanted. Although I am strong, I also asked God to support me during this upcoming time.

I felt an odd sense of being gratefully scared.

Toward the end of the second day, I started to convince myself I was okay and I wasn't hooked. Although I didn't feel great, I thought a little help in the form of a laced cigarette wouldn't hurt anything. But I didn't listen to this voice. It was at that moment that I realized I probably was hooked because the voice kept coming back, again and again. It seemed so innocent at first until it began to change its tone and tenor as time went by. Each time I said "no" the voice became more forceful, begging me to not head into the dark hole lying just ahead.

About day four into this dance of asking and saying no, I was a very sick puppy. My mind swam with wild, hallucinatory dreams and my body ached everywhere. Chills and an acute fever crawled through me. My head and aching body screamed for relief from all this dark, deep pain, and all the while my addiction kept telling me "Just one hit, one puff, and all this pain will go away."

Sweating profusely in the hot, humid Vietnamese air, I lay there in delirious states of awakening, death-like trances, hearing the call of the addiction, and with a very physical pain clawing at and under my skin. It was as if my insides were crawling to the surface of my skin and wanting out. The experience must be the "cold turkey" experience people talked about when someone kicks an addiction such as mine without the soft landing of transitory drugs.

My friends were terrific at keeping vigil over me. Whenever they came by, I tried to convince them I was "good" and they could leave. Their persistent showing up day after day, hour after hour, was a blessing. Monky, who might have seen this before, didn't honor my request that she stay away. Every day she would show up and spend hours wiping my brow, neck, and back with cloths soaked in fresh water as I lay there. She was like my guardian protector.

Then one day I woke up, and it was as if I had part of my life back. Something had shifted. I had crossed a river, and although I was still wet, I'd made it across. The addiction was again calling out to me, tempting me, but it appeared that I had it under my control and I could say "no" more easily. It was then I knew I was going to go home clean.

Chapter 7

Standing on a Cliff

Staying clean from heroin for 18 years has been relatively easy because of the people in my life and my determination to control my life and live sober. But here I was, sitting on a log during this Big Sur journey, still struggling and chaffing at my nagging desire to be free from my inner demons. Why wasn't I feeling free and living joyfully?

I looked out at the meadow sloping down to the cliff and the ocean beyond, and the realization hit me: I was losing the war inside me. No, I was not happy with my life. I'd answered this question truthfully.

Sadness crawled around inside my body, the depression of not having the kind of life I had dreamed and envisioned for myself. I had hoped to be happily married, wealthy, a great person doing important work. I had expected to have embodied inner peace, not inner anguish.

Instead, for all the work I'd done, inside and out, here I was standing in a meadow feeling that I'd betrayed myself. Maybe expectations were killing me.

"How did I get so unhappy?" was the next question I heard myself ask. Smiling sarcastically, I answered with a question, "When was I ever happy; I mean truly and fully pleased with who I was?" An image of my adopted daughter, Michelle, came to me and I smiled. Whenever I thought of her trusting me with the role and name of "Daddy" I felt incredible joy and happiness powered by love. Thinking of my daughter always made me feel as if a warm arrow was piercing my heart.

I met Michelle between my tours of Vietnam. She was only a month and a half old when I saw her for the very first time. Her mother, Susan S., had invited me over to see Michelle while I was home on my 30-day leave. I had known Susan through most of high school, and as friends, we had run with the same group of people back then. When I walked into Susan's house, there was Michelle on a baby blanket near the dining room, looking so innocent, small, and beautiful. Picking her up, holding her, brought a rush of joy—here I was holding new life—and pain and sadness: my job in Vietnam had been to take away lives, and in a few short days I'd be back killing people again.

When I got out of the Army on May 25, 1971, adjusting to civilian life didn't always work well. Whenever I heard a sudden loud banging noise, I would duck my head or fall flat to the ground in a swift, jerky motion. It seemed as if I was always looking around, looking for something that wasn't right. I walked with caution. One time, driving in my VW camper van, I heard a car backfire near me and suddenly found myself with my head against the center of the steering wheel and the van up on the traffic island in the middle of the four-lane boulevard. My knuckles were white from my panicked grip on the steering wheel. I was ungrounded and skittish. To deal with this stress and the unwelcoming way Vietnam veterans were treated, I took some small camping trips and even did a two-and-a-half-month trek through Europe.

In the fall of 1971, five months after getting out of the Army, I started classes at Orange Coast College, a junior college in Costa Mesa, California. Although I'd wanted to go to a regular four-year college, my dismal high school academics only qualified me for a JC, which anybody could attend. I also began dating Susan. Every time I was with her and Michelle I felt more grounded, more a member of the world and life.

Susan and I came from different backgrounds but raised in similar ways. I wasn't seen for who I was, and I don't believe she was either. Her father, Art, was a former Navy Seal and although he had an incredibly soft heart for little Michelle, he could be one tough SOB. He and I were a real-life version of the characters, Archie and Mike, in the television program *All in the Family*. We had distinctly different ways of looking at life, his being pro-military and mine antiwar. Even so, we shared an obvious caring through our mutual love for Susan and Michelle. Susan's mom, Anne, was pleasant but I always got the feeling that Art ran the show. Susan had Michelle as a single mother right out of high school. In those days, it was difficult for a young woman to be an unmarried mother living at home with her parents; it was not an ideal situation for Susan.

For me, it was a gift, because the more time I spent with both Susan and Michelle, the more confidence I gained that there was a purpose for me and my daily, growing, unconditional, protective love for Michelle. Although my love might have been a sliver of Susan's motherly love for her amazing daughter, I wanted to be a part of her life forever.

I'd rented a small studio apartment and taken a job as a machinist at Wells Marine, a company that milled and fabricated metal products. One of Wells Marine's customers was the U.S. government, for which it made dummy bullet shell casings. I worked on two substantial Conomatic Automatic Screw machines that took eight 20-foot long steel bars and methodically cut them into 4-inch-long machined segments. While being bathed in cutting oil, the parts were cut with chamfers on the outer edges and simultaneously hollowed out the center. The machine did all this to exact specifications, then cut the product off into a basket. My job was to shove the steel bars into the end of the machine, quality-check the final cut products, and adjust the cutting tools to keep the product within specifications.

Each day, after spending four to six hours in class, I'd head out to Wells Marine and work my 4:00 PM to midnight shift. When I came home, I'd spend an hour getting the cutting oil off my body and out of my clothes. I was focused on getting good grades and keeping myself out of debt, so I studied a lot and worked hard.

My respite came on weekends as I found myself spending more and more time with Susan and Michelle. Going to the park on a Saturday or Sunday and playing with Michelle by pushing her on a swing or playing in the sandbox was extraordinarily grounding, making me feel alive. I embraced being with a beautiful young spirit who was helping me engage with life. Michelle kept me from becoming depressed over the amount of work I was trying to accomplish to make my life better.

One day near her second birthday she finally decided that she wanted to try the big kids slide at the park. She loved the small slide. The thrill of coming down it made her laugh out loud. Her fascination with the big kid's slide was always overshadowed, however, by its height. From her point of view, the stairs up to the platform must have looked like a ladder to the sky.

Today would be different. Michelle put her foot on the first step, then the second, and with me right behind her feeling very protective, she made her way, step by step, to the top. Each time she hesitated, my continued reassurance allowed her to keep putting one foot in front of the other. When we reached the top, she sat down on the platform. I told her, "Hold on right here" as I placed her little hands on each of the metal side rails, "I'm going to climb down the stairs and catch you as you come down the slide." She turned and looked at me anxiously. "Don't worry," I said, "I'll catch you." Michelle looked at me with a slight bit of skepticism and fear, but she said "Okay."

As I crouched at the bottom of the slide, she kept her blue eyes on me anxiously, seeming to hesitate at the thought of letting go. "We're going to count to three and on 'three' you let go," I said to her. Together we said, "One, two, three." Her hands let go, and her arms flew up, and she sped down the metal face. Halfway down she looked at me, and I could see that she knew I'd be there for her. She smiled, let out a laugh, and as she barreled into my protective embrace she looked up and said, "Again!"

The joy of this memory will always be with me. At that moment I knew I would be there for her for the rest of her life. I also felt that she knew this, that she let herself go to love me as the primary male figure in her life and that she knew I'd do what it took to be her daddy.

One weekend, unceremoniously, Susan and I drove to Las Vegas and were married.

Having Michelle in my life created the space within me to think and act in ways that were for another and not just for myself. One Saturday evening, after studying all day and Susan headed off to work, I got out my stash of pot and rolled a joint. After smoking it, I picked up my guitar and started to tune it. Because it was an inexpensive guitar, it wouldn't tune accurately or correctly, so in playing chords, I would spend time finding the best compromise setting. Tonight, probably because I was very high, I couldn't find the ideal spot for each string, and I spent almost two hours trying to tune the instrument.

Finally, I gave up, set the guitar down, and went into Michelle's bedroom to check on her. Seeing this angel of my life in her bed softly breathing, I became overwhelmed by the immensity of raising a child. Then I started to tear up, overwhelmed by this responsibility. I couldn't tune a guitar, let alone raise a child.

I walked back into the living room and over to the bookshelf where I'd hidden my stash of pot and pills. Opening the small box, I thought, "This must end." Taking it into the bathroom, I dumped its contents into the toilet and flushed it. Watching the ground leaves of my pot along with a few pills swirl down and disappear allowed me to think that maybe I had a chance to be a better parent.

Upon reflection, with the clarity of hindsight, I know I married Susan more to be Michelle's dad than to be a husband. Still, I did love Susan. We were not compatible in many ways. However, I am profoundly and eternally grateful to Susan for supporting me in adopting Michelle as my daughter. By comparison, all other moments of joy and happiness that I'd experienced—landing a new job, receiving a raise, finding a new girlfriend, a new car, a new place to live, even another marriage—seemed only momentary and fleeting.

Our differences in lifestyle, values, and my infidelity are what ended our marriage, although we both ensured Michelle felt loved by both parents.

The fleeting feeling of joy of my first marriage was similerly duplicated in my second marriage and subsequent divorce. Dominica H. was someone I'd see almost every time I went to a racquetball club that was just around the corner from my Pleasant Hill apartment nestled in the San Francisco East Bay. She worked behind the front check-in desk. Long before asymmetrical haircuts were in fashion, she had one, with close-cropped on the left side and long, curly, flowing locks on her right. I'd say "Hi!" and she responded in kind through her open, beautiful smile. Even though she might be busy with several other people wanting to check in, it seemed as though she took an extra moment to give me her direct attention. I felt a flush when she did this. When I finally got the guts to ask her to lunch one day, she said, "Yes!" with excitement. We went to a small, cute place she liked and from there we began a wild, whirlwind romance that ended up six months later in a beautiful Berkeley Rose Garden wedding. Although this was my second marriage, I was hopeful that my rushing into it was not to fulfill a need to be loved but to embrace a relationship that was genuine in all ways.

I had a habit of making snap decisions without first learning about someone. In this case, I learned within a couple of months after our marriage that Dominica was bulimic. From that moment on, I fell into caretaker mode, which she both liked and resented. We went through therapy, she signed up for a residential eating-disorder program, and I went to a corresponding support group, plus a personal therapist. On New Year's Eve day, less than six months after our wedding, I came home from work to find a note from Dominica. She was leaving to find herself and gain confidence that she could be free of her eating disorder, alone. Shortly afterward, we jointly filed for an uncontested divorce.

Although I was partially heartbroken, the therapy helped me to see behaviors that were not helpful to my well-being. Once again, I re-focused on work and career.

Shortly after our divorce, I bought my townhome. As with many other moments, acquiring the house produced intense feelings of happiness and joy that dissolved within a day or two, to be taken over by a lurking sense of dissatisfaction. I had enjoyed my last job; but I had still experienced it as "work," not "happiness."

So here I was on this camping trip wondering if being happy was predetermined, a matter of fate, or if it was earned, or learned. I speculated about; were we born happy and some of us learn to be unhappy, or if we are born unhappy, and some of us learn to be satisfied, or if we are born neither happy nor unhappy and grow into either unhappiness or happiness. It seemed to me that there were more unhappy people than happy people in the world, but then I had only a small sample from a couple of countries and cultures.

Strolling toward the ocean, I felt the fresh, brisk, salty air remind me of being grateful that my Vietnam heroin experience had taught me that there probably are no drugs I could take to make this emptiness go away.

I recalled reading a Buddhist text about a Sanskrit term *Pretas*. *Pretas* represents Hungry Ghosts, an unending emptiness that cannot be fulfilled. That fitted my feeling. These ghosts are teardrop-shaped with very bloated stomachs and slender, thin limbs. The mouth of a hungry ghost is a small, elongated opening. Passing food through this mouth to fill a hungry ghost's distended stomachs is painfully slow.

Hungry ghosts can never get enough food to allow those distended stomachs to feel full. Of course, hungry ghosts represent a constant effort to fill oneself up but never feeling contented. They spend their whole lives trying to consume more and more, but it is never enough.

I felt like one of these ghosts. I had been attempting to fill my life up with things as a way to become happier and more successful. The partial proof was my four-level, three-bedroom, 2½ bath townhome with plenty of furniture and my two cars in the garage while I eyed another, third, vehicle—and I was the only person living there. Yes, I could be a hungry ghost.

I had eaten lunch at the top of the knoll with the expanse of the Big Sur coastline laid out below me. Looking south, I saw a line of trees bordering a fence stretching down to the cliff edge. Slowly turning my face west and then north, I looked along the cliff edge to a far distant, jagged peninsula sticking out from the cliff line. I felt the air leave my lungs in a defeated way as if I was resigning myself to despair. Looking for the trail toward the cliff, I spied it directly west about 50 feet away. I lifted my right foot, placed it in front of my left, and kept walking.

Trudging down the gentle slope, I found the well-worn path and began winding my way through the calf-high, dry coastal bush. About a half mile into the trail I came to a fork. One of the splits headed due north, parallel to the cliff edge and about an eighth of a mile inland, while the other path directed straight west toward the cliff edge.

I decided to head west, hoping that the trail eventually turned north and up the coastline back toward the campground. If it didn't, I could always backtrack to the other path and follow it back to my tent.

After deciding to head down toward the cliff, I felt my body and mind slip away into a walking zombie state in which I was paying little attention to where I was walking, just watching the distant rows of waves head toward shore.

Thoughts drifted in and out of my head. The word "happiness" kept popping up. Was happiness a temporary state of mind existing when certain conditions were met and prevailed? Or was it available as a constant even while one was experiencing the ups and downs of life? I'd run across people who claimed to be happy all the time even when they were going through difficult times. I'd seen them shrug off the small tics life brings and become emotional when massive tragedies befell them. Through each of these types of events, they claimed to be happy.

Still, others said they were unhappy regardless of the number of negative or positive events in their lives. So, it seemed that some people appeared to be happy or unhappy, no matter what befell them, and others were happy for brief moments.

"Why is my mind thinking about these things?" I asked out loud to the wind. I wondered if others besides me think about the complexities of happiness at some point in their lives. While I understood that none of us experiences happiness in quite the same way, I couldn't help wondering if my experience was unique. I smiled as a line from one of Paul Simon's songs came to me, "One man's ceiling is another man's floor."

I resigned to never getting an answer on what happiness is for others. Even so, I believe it helped me to ask the question, if only to become aware that the answer is ultimately unknowable.

Returning my focus to my own experience of happiness, I sat down to watch the ocean. As I did, another question arose in my mind. This one more metaphorical: If I were a boat out there on the water, and the peaks and valleys of waves were the highs and lows of my life, would happiness be an ability to float on top of these experiences, to ride on top of these peaks and valleys buoyantly without sinking? Or would happiness be found if my boat was affixed on a solid foundation, anchored as it were, to a vertical pole in the water so that the rising and falling waves would put me either underwater or high and dry? Or, stating this second choice differently, would I find happiness in the security of being affixed in one spot and gratefully accepting the waves of life, even when they rolled over me? Maybe neither of these images offered me an answer to happiness. Floating buoyantly on life's ups and downs might not allow for a deeper understanding. Alternatively, being fixed in one place could mean an inability to let go and experience the flow of life. Maybe the metaphorical key to happiness lay in how I related to the boat itself, and how it interacted with the ocean it rested on.

Walking again, I stepped over grey granite rocks and zigzagged between bushes on the dirt trail as I gazed out toward the ocean, pondering these questions.

The trail grew circuitous, and I stopped looking at the ocean and focused on the dirt path right in front of me. Carefully making my way toward the cliff's edge, I thought about my happiness or the lack thereof and wondered if it was a symptom of something more profound. Suddenly, the thoughts I had had earlier in the day while picking up sticks of wood and my feelings about being a boat on the ocean rolled together into one final view: maybe happiness is being satisfied, embracing, or accepting what I have at every moment. In other words, perhaps happiness merely is recognizing what is as *what is*.

The roar of the ocean below echoed in my ears as I approached the edge of the cliff. The sound of waves crashing against the rugged rocks a good 200 to 300 feet below brought back many memories. I had lived very near, or within a few miles of the water, most of my life and the sound of the waves hitting the shore felt like home.

Recollections of growing up in Redondo Beach, CA and going to the beach began to flow through my mind. I smiled with the remembrance of being a four-year-old thrown about by the waves while fearlessly clinging to a rubber surf mat with my dad's words ringing in my ears as he pushed me down the face of another wave, "Don't let go!" I recalled learning how to body surf and how close I felt to the power of the ocean as I slid down its face, eyes open while guiding myself away from the breaking curl. Then I recalled building my first surfboard by hand in my pre-teenage years and taking it out for the first time. After that came memories of my high school years when my friends and I went to the beach to surf, meet girls, and sit around campfires at night drinking whatever alcohol we could get our hands on.

I watched the spray of the water as it hit the rocks. I've always liked to watch the ocean, especially when it was hitting rocks, amazed that each time a wave would slam the same stone, the spray was still different.

Now here I stood on the edge of this cliff drinking in all the sounds, smells, and sights that the ocean offered. My thoughts and memories became frosting on the cake of this suddenly spectacular scene. I was eating it up, and for a moment I felt happy, free, and alive.

My thoughts then turned back to my morning, the question, about being happy and the resulting answer. Nearly half of my expected life was gone, and I couldn't say that I was pleased.

My earlier despair flooded back, and a strange sensation came over me. Pulled closer to the edge, nudged by a hollow place, the hungry ghost in my stomach, the edge of the cliff was my invitation.

The beautiful slow rolling movement of the waves starting from the horizon and moving toward shore was hypnotic. They kept rolling forward, then ended their lives with a violent collision against the jagged rock cliffs below. Was this going to be my fate as well? Was I going to end up crashing onto the rocks as well?

"What do I need to do to be happy?" I asked myself. My mind went immediately toward getting a new job, but then I realized this would just be doing more of the same, just like picking up the firewood earlier in the day, just looking for something better when all that seemed to do was bring me dissatisfaction and dropping one piece for another seemingly better piece. Exasperated, my mind started spinning on about what was this life all about anyway. Feelings of unhappiness, loneliness, sadness, confusion, and wondering about the meaning of life, wondering about my life, arose as I stood on the cliff's edge. Getting a new job wouldn't change this and

I knew it. What I needed was a different perspective, a different view, maybe just a different mind. Something had to change.

My hopelessness grew as I stood there. Looking over the edge of the cliff, I knew that I could take one more tiny step and all of this pain would go away. It all would be over. Tears welled up and fell down my cheeks. I wanted this pain and sadness to end and stepping off the cliff would do it. I imagined my family's reaction. "How could he do this?" "He was always troubled." "How did we miss this?" Or maybe just, "What happened?"

I looked over the edge. The rocks looked hard and at the same time inviting. The argument of whether or not to jump churned in my head and stomach. I certainly didn't want to live in this confusion, sadness, and pain any longer. I was tired of living a life that felt stuck, meaningless, and unhappy.

Indecision rolled in and out of my mind and body, like the waves below. One moment I was ready to jump and the next moment I couldn't. Questions about what to change and how to change it raced faster and faster through my mind.

The cold wind hitting my face made my tears even colder. My cheeks were tight from previously dried tears. The hole in my stomach kept expanding and contracting with each quick decision of "change" or "jump."

"Decide now," I said in an angry-with-myself voice toward the ocean and to the sky.

What was keeping me from changing? Not knowing what to change and what would make a difference. Even if I had an idea of what to change, would I know how? If I had to change everything in my life, what would my new life look like, and would it be any better than the experience I was having? I wondered about my family and if they would or wouldn't accept me if I changed. If I lived a life that was different from the way they raised me, would I be recognized? I wondered if it would even matter. And my daughter, what would she think? Would I become the worst dad ever?

One thing I knew. None of my friends or family would be happy if I killed myself. But then, I wouldn't have to hear about it, nor would I care. I'd be gone.

The sun was starting to set, and I realized that I'd been standing there for over two hours. I had to decide and decide now. Step forward or step back.

As tears continued to flow down my face, I took a deep breath. I need to decide now. Then my body decided. My right foot lifted and stepped back. I was going to change how I lived my life, even if I had to change everything.

Chapter 8

Goodbye to Home

As I backed away from the cliff's edge, my stomach began to relax and let me breathe again. Only half the sun was above the dark blue ocean horizon which meant it would be getting dark soon. The light lengthened the shadows of the bushes around me. The color of the coastal vegetation took on a slight golden hue. With each step, my breathing became more relaxed and fuller. I saw that the path along the cliff was clear of vegetation and wide enough to follow after sunset, so I knew that I'd be able to get back to my tent without much of a problem.

Questions bombarded me about what I would have to change. Fear of the unknown washed over me. My mind rapidly considered alternative lifestyles and wondered how I would find and live them. I stopped for a moment and looked at the trail at my feet. "Just take another step," I mumbled to myself. "Take another step," as if a higher spirit was guiding me.

Why couldn't I focus entirely on taking one more step followed by another? As usual, my mind was making the straightforward action of wanting to resolve and fix everything. Like I was in a race to complete every possible task I could think of ahead of time. Why did I think I had to get stuff done now as if there was an end to get to? Couldn't I take the next step and enjoy the journey? "Breathe…" I said softly to myself elongating the "eeee" part of the word. "Take another step."

The trail descended toward a beach through a series of switchbacks where a small river flowed into the ocean. The light was moving into dusk, or "magic time" as it's sometimes called in the movie business because filming at this time, the light appears on film more like night and shadows are less pronounced. During this time the blue wavelength light is more prominent in the sky while red and yellow wavelength light surges in the horizon with sheer beauty. Reaching the bottom of the trail, I sat down on a log next to the river, took off my hiking boots, rolled up my Levi's, and waded across the river to where the trail picked up again.

Putting my socks on my wet feet and sliding on my boots, I thought about how refreshingly cool the water felt. Tying the last lace, I looked up at the medium-blue light on the western horizon shading up to deeper blue above. This magical moment of the darkening sky gave me a surge of peace. I watched as the medium blue turned to the indigo of night with a sprinkling of stars becoming visible in the darker eastern sky. I'd forgotten how much I loved this time of the evening.

In Carlos Castaneda's *The Teachings of Don Juan*, Don Juan says that this demarcation, the space between day and night, is an opening or crack in the universe through which one can leap into the truth. I saw that crack open for me that evening.

As I made my way down the last half-mile of the trail, I could hear the river on my right as it moved over rocks and partially submerged logs. I set my backpack down next to my tent and checked the area for other campers.

At the opposite end of the meadow about a quarter mile away, a fire glowed next to a small tent. Another camper, I thought. Now there were two tents on this spacious coastal campground. By this time, the night was completely dark, and the stars were out in full force. It didn't appear that there would be any wind tonight; everything seemed calm. I opened my food storage bin, grabbed some wheat crackers, cheese, and dried ramen noodles, and set them on one of the granite rocks of the fire pit. Then I occupied myself with building a campfire, using my carefully chosen wood, to heat water for noodles. I found that I'd fallen into a nice rhythm, a welcome change after such an emotional and tumultuous day.

After my meal, I sat beside the crackling fire, sipping some hot water, and began to collect my thoughts on today's events. What a day this was! I had come close to ending my life, yet I had chosen to live.

This was not the first time I had wanted to stop living. I tried to take my life early in 1978 after two years after my first divorce and experience another failure at developing a relationship and screwed by a business partner in a new business I'd created. Instead of a cliff, I had chosen to take a half-dozen pills from a bottle of old pain medication I had lying around. After ingesting the pills, I got very woozy, stumbled toward the bathroom, and awoke later with my face in a puddle of vomit on the carpet floor.

That event hadn't changed my life, so today I was unsure if the changes I'd committed to would make a difference. For now, I was content to watch the flames dance toward the night sky and begin a meditation that would help me slip into a sound night's sleep.

The next morning, I did notice one thing. I felt strangely different from how I'd felt the day before as if a huge load was lifted off my back.

My remaining 12 days of camping consisted of reflective hikes, meditations, and watching nature unfold before me. One morning, I watched a couple of young sparrow hawks with their mother hunt for food. I was mesmerized by their ability to hover and carefully watch a particular area. For hours on end, I watched their hovering, darting, and soaring over the meadow until at one point one of the hawks dived and captured a lizard. I was amazed by their natural persistence and focus on seeking and catching food.

On the last day of this trip, I awoke early in the morning to find a moist fog clinging to the ground. Most of my stuff was wet with moisture from the mist, so I decided to wait to pack. Because I had put away most of the cooking utensils the previous night, I hiked down the path to the car and drove into Big Sur, found a restaurant, and enjoyed an excellent breakfast. I picked up a newspaper and attempted to catch up on the news of the world while sipping my coffee. I didn't notice any anxiousness about leaving, and I wasn't obsessing about what my next step would be. Finishing my coffee and reading the paper *was* my next step. The more substantial actions would have to wait until I got home. Then I'd have enough time and possibly some new clues to what would be next in my life. I was clear, however, that my goal was to be willing to change everything in the way I lived.

Returning to the campground, I found the fog was gone and my equipment dry. I packed everything into two loads that I could carry to the parking lot about a mile away without overloading myself.

With the car packed and my stomach tightening a bit from the knowledge that I was heading back out into the world as a somewhat different person, I gave a slight bow in the direction of the campground and another one toward the hillside trail where I had made an important decision 13 days ago. When I started the car, a new-found bit of excitement stirred within me, a sense of hope, a possibility of a new way, a new life.

The drive home was uneventful. Mostly I scanned the roadside to see if anything had changed. As I pulled into my garage, I got a powerful and clear feeling that this home would tie me down. "Sell the home," I told myself. It was my first explicit action thought.

More action thoughts quickly followed. First, as I unloaded the camping gear and put it away, I started seeing all the stuff I owned. Two of the bedrooms were furnished with bedroom furniture, while the third served as a home office and meditation room. The master bedroom was on its level, the highest in the house, and had a enormous and long bathroom with two sinks, shower, separate bath area, and a huge walk-in closet. Each room had a full complement of furniture, and I had been acquiring more and more stuff, most of which I rarely used. I generally worked 10 to 12 hours a day, and with my commute of an hour each way to the city and back, I was rarely home.

I turned on the heater to warm up the cold house and walked up the stairs to take a shower and hop into bed. I was tired. I hadn't slept in my bed in two weeks. The trip had been emotional and stressful. Walking into my bedroom, I felt a part of me saying goodbye to this room and the things in it. Now that I had decided to sell the house, I started thinking about what I would do with all the furniture and stuff. I opened the shower door, reached in, and turned the handle to the left, releasing a stream of hot water. Sliding into the flow of warm, soothing water from the showerhead, my thoughts and worries circled gently down the drain between my feet. There is nothing like the feeling of a nice shower to wash away nagging thoughts.

As I toweled down my body, I could feel the sensation of anxiousness begin to replace the water I was drying off. I put on old, comfortable sweater and sweatpants and headed to my meditation room to sit, let go of my thoughts, and hopefully relax and ready myself for bed.

The next morning, my first thought was to find a real estate agent and to outline what to do with my belongings. After a moderately effective workout at the local gym, I went home and called some friends who had experience with local agents.

One thing was clear. I wasn't going to be selling my home in the best of markets. It was a buyers' market, and after I paid off the mortgage, fees, and commission, I'd have very little cash remaining.

Even so, my home had become an albatross around my neck. I wanted to create possibilities, as many as possible, and doing this meant selling it.

Chapter 9

The SAGE Experience

"It's done!" The words echoed off the walls of the empty entry area and living room. My home looked as if no one had ever lived here. It was emptied, the barren walls of the house were washed and scrubbed. Some of my furniture and possessions had moved to a small transition apartment in Larkspur overlooking the ferry terminal, and the rest of my stuff found its way to Goodwill Industries, was sold, or given away to friends or family. I no longer existed in that space.

I kept the larger of the two cars, a 1989 white Ford Taurus, brand new and paid for, and sold the older, less practical, two-seat Pontiac Fiero. When I started up the Taurus, the empty walls of the garage reverberated with the sound of the engine.

I looked up over the steering wheel, then the rear-view mirror and glanced over my right shoulder to ease the car out of the garage one last time. Once out of the garage, I got out of the car and clicked the garage door button. The grinding sound of the closing garage door broke the silent morning air. I dropped the garage door remote into the locked mailbox, gave one last look at the front door, and drove away.

My first act after leaving the world of home ownership was to drive to A Clean Well-Lighted Place for Books, a bookstore and café near my transition apartment, for a double espresso. Again, the thought flashed through my mind: I had no idea what I would be doing next.

The thick, dark smell of the double espresso was powerfully pleasant, and its rich, almost bitter taste grounded me. The coffee itself gave me new energy, enough to start thinking slightly into the future, beginning with now. I picked up *The Wall Street Journal* and started scanning the articles, partly to lessen my anxiety and partly to gain information about the state of the world around me and what people were thinking. Then I turned to the Opportunities section. Would my next step be there, written in an advertisement?

One never knows where and when the next opportunity might arise. In the mid-1980's, before getting my latest job, I was watching television and flipping through the channels when I came across an infomercial promoting personal and financial success. The program, *Personal Power* by Tony Robbins, was offered on audio tapes. It pushed and promised that if you do the exercises presented in the recordings, you will be happy and have financial success. Watching Tony speak and show video clips of his in-person seminars, which he was also promoting, I was entranced by the energy of his presentation. "Maybe I could do that," I said to myself while watching him energetically command his audience in the clips—and me in my living room. I wondered how I could use my intelligence, compassion, and desire to help others in the same way he was doing. Also, I liked the idea of being publicly successful.

After buying the tapes and diligently practicing the exercises and techniques, I believe that following Tony's program contributed to me getting my most recent job, one that paid very well and that I'd liked.

As I read *The Journal's* Opportunities section, I could see I wasn't qualified for most of them. Then something caught my eye: an ad for motivational speakers. "Speak and Grow Rich," it said. You can make money being a motivational speaker helping people find their path to success. The sponsor of the ad was SAGE Seminars. The message stayed with me while I read the rest of the paper.

As I finished my double espresso, my mind kept calling me back to the ad and its promise of helping people to become more successful. I paged back to the Opportunities section and re-read the text. Using the edge of my pen, I cut out the ad and put it in my pocket.

The next morning, I called the number in the advertisement and listened to a three- to the four-minute message that talked about making internal changes through choices, resourcing, love, and self-actualization. The recording touched me in a place I hadn't acknowledged for many years. The last time I had explicitly thought of these things was studying Social Ecology at the University of California, Irvine while working with Dr. Peter Welgan doing biofeedback research in the field of psychophysiology. The message ended with a request for the caller to leave a summary of their skills, experience with seminars, and why they would be an excellent candidate to be a motivational and personal growth instructor.

I froze, and my mind went blank, so I quickly hung up the phone. I felt exposed because the message spoke of things that were inwardly important and powerful to me, things I hadn't acknowledged or acted upon in years.

I didn't know what to say that would be reflective of me, my interests and qualifications, and impress the staff at SAGE. I took a moment to collect my thoughts, then wrote down a set of points I wanted to cover. I knew it would be essential to leave a short and concise recording, so I practiced it a couple of times. After dialing the number, I waited for the tone and said, "The subjects you spoke of in your message touched my heart and brought me back to my college days when I studied human behavior and how people both resist and accept change. I feel as though I have the intelligence and abilities to communicate personal growth to people in a more formal context." I included my callback number and hung up the phone.

Soon I had a call back from a woman named Josephine M. At first, I was unimpressed with what Josephine had to say because it felt as though she was feeding me just what she assumed I wanted to hear. She came across—maybe partly because of her Brooklyn accent—as wanting to sell me something. I reacted the way I do when I'm at an automobile dealership and evident I'm being led down a path where I'm soon going to be asked, "What would it take for you to drive out with this car today?" Josephine seemed determined to convince me how full of integrity and honesty the people in SAGE were. That was a warning sign to me. If people need to tell you they're honest, then it might be essential to keep an eye open. I also could feel a sales pitch coming, and I was waiting for Josephine to make the pitch.

I was surprised, however, when she said, "Why don't you come down to our free two-hour preview in Emeryville this Thursday night?" Emeryville is a hotel- and mall-filled town bordering the San Francisco Bay west of Berkeley, 35 minutes from my home in Larkspur. That, I thought, was easy enough to do. I'd been to a small number of personal growth previews in my day, including hardcore presentations by *est* (Erhard Seminars Training and Latin for "it is"), so I knew what to expect, including a pitch for enrollment. I certainly knew how to say "no."

"Sure," I said, "I'd be happy to join you."

I arrived at the hotel about 15 minutes early and entered a nearly empty meeting room. Three people were sitting in the middle of the room, and another four huddled at its front. I surmised that the group at the front of the room must be with SAGE. A heavy-set woman left the group and introduced herself. It was Josephine, in a loose-fitting black and gold clothing with an overabundance of gold-colored jewelry on her wrists, fingers, and neck. She said, "The presentation will begin soon. Have a seat." She probably sensed that I was about to leave. As I sat down, one of the other SAGE people started speaking to us, attendees. He said that his experience with SAGE had thus far been life-changing and that for the first time he had felt able to understand his actions and to participate in the world more clearly. When he finished his story, he announced the next speaker, Bill Dempsey, founder of SAGE.

Bill was short, stocky, barrel-chested and a bit overweight. He had thick, grey, curly hair and a round, friendly, joyful face. After explaining that SAGE was an acronym for Self Actualization Growth Exploration, Bill spoke at length of his experience in personal growth seminars. Besides working with Werner Erhard of *est*, his past affiliations included the founders of Silva Mind Control, Mind Dynamics, and Leadership Dynamics and ESP with Jose Silva, Alexander Everett, and William Penn Patrick, respectively. After this recitation of his credentials, intended to impress us with his qualifications for creating SAGE, Bill began to speak about the money-making opportunities SAGE could provide to its enlistees. I caught only some of the details, but in essence, if you became a "Sage Master" by taking and passing their series of seminars, you could purchase geographical area rights to produce and deliver SAGE Dreamwalk seminars.

The presentation wasn't very compelling, and I'm sure the members of SAGE who were in the room noticed my reaction. After the performance, as I was standing up to head out the door, Josephine stopped by and asked me if I would like to meet one of their current Sage Masters.

That person was James W., a chiropractor in San Francisco and the East Bay. He started sharing how much he had "got" about himself by attending the SAGE seminar series. He told me that he was committed to completing the training program so that he could present "Dreamwalk" seminars, SAGE's basic public course. We spoke about some of the things he had gotten from the seminars. They consisted mostly of a better understanding of his "subconscious programs," how they affected his day-to-day life, and learning to begin releasing them to better come from a place of authenticity.

When I asked James about the business aspect of the role, he told me he thought his $10,000 investment would be a good one because James believed a lot of people would want to have the experience he was having with SAGE.

"I think people want to grow and become more self-actualized," he said, "and by offering these seminars to 100 or so people two or three times a month, I'll make a lot of money. At $295.00 a head, each seminar could generate more than $29K."

"That's a lot of money," I replied, "and from what I heard today I find it hard to believe that the seminars are all that powerful. But I could be wrong."

Josephine interrupted at that point. She said that there was a free half-day meeting next Saturday at a different hotel in Emeryville and that it would begin to show me the power of the SAGE seminars. She gave me a flyer for the location and time of this introductory meeting. What did I have to lose?

This time, I arrived at the meeting about 20 minutes before its scheduled 10:00 a.m. kick-off and saw a situation out of control. People were arguing with each other about room layout, the hotel didn't seem to be cooperating, and nobody seemed to be in charge. After waiting 45 minutes, the session was already about 25 minutes late, and I was ready to leave. Just as I walked out the door toward the elevator, someone popped out into the hall and said: "we're ready now, why don't you have a seat."

By now I was skeptical of this entirely amateur operation, but I thought, "What the hell." Back inside, attendants were eagerly guiding the 25 to 30 people to seats. I smiled to myself, thinking I must have been sporting my don't-screw-with-me look because none of them attempted to direct me to a specific place.

The meeting started with a guy named Richard W., who indicated he was a Sage Master from Southern California who had been successfully putting on Dreamwalk seminars for six months. He began by introducing people who had taken various SAGE courses. Each of them got up and told their story starting with a summary of disillusionment after which they segued to how SAGE seminars changed them. A couple of these speakers were dressed in business suits and had worked in the corporate world, as I had so that I could relate to their stories. Their former worlds were like the world I just left behind.

During the mid-day break, I connected with a man named Michael B. Earlier we had done a dyad exercise together. A dyad is a structured communication exercise between two people; sometimes it is used during corporate training. Michael was slightly shorter than I, wore glasses, and in our brief encounter seemed very thoughtful and intelligent. As the two of us chatted about our past experiences and history, we discovered that we had a lot in common. We both had many of the same questions regarding the SAGE business model and decided to meet after this preview to discuss our mutual matters in more depth.

When we returned to the seminar room, Richard was introducing Simon W. as the next presenter. As one of SAGE's senior teachers, Richard explained that Simon was a therapist and healer who specialized in a process called "resourcing." He explained to us that "resourcing" consists of Simon working intimately with someone to "dis-create" negative programming. He does this, Richard said, by using "a combination of rebirthing, empathy, clairvoyance, and a large measure of caring."

Simon had an air of clarity about and around him. His bald head and skinny frame made him look frail, but his intense, bright eyes belied this delicate look. Simon explained that during this session he would be sitting facing or next to a subject and would be asking simple questions such as "How are you doing?" or "What are you feeling?" The subject could respond with something like "I'm feeling nervous." Simon would then begin to direct the subject's energy toward the truth by telling him or her to say, "I'm feeling nervous because..." and complete the sentence. It might go something like "I'm feeling nervous because I'm feeling exposed in front of all these people." If Simon sensed that the response was an excuse or a way to deflect a deeper response, he would redirect the subject by saying something like, "That's not quite true. Try again. I'm feeling nervous because...."

Simon made it clear that if he sensed that the person's response was accurate or heading down a more profound path, he would repeat the person's statement—for example, "You don't like sharing yourself in front of people because you feel they're judging you." The subject would be asked to repeat this phrase and reply with a more candid response. With each response that succeeded in more honestly expressing a core issue, Simon would continue to guide the subject toward the point. When, at last, the core issue is discovered in full, there would be a moment of clarity that would be visible to the audience and emotively felt by Simon and the subject.

Simon assured us that under his gentle, intuitive guidance each subject would begin to realize the pretense from which an issue is created. By getting to the behavior's core roots, the matter would then start to "dis-create the negative program."

I had an inkling that Simon would be asking for a volunteer, and knowing my willingness and propensity to try new things, I knew I'd raise my hand and volunteer. I've learned that for me to get something at a deep level, I need to experience it, even if it means doing it in front of strangers. Having had some public speaking experience, I know that I'm usually comfortable in that role. I had always been willing to put myself out there in front of people.

When Simon asked for volunteers, one other person and I raised our hands. Simon selected me, and I moved to the chair next to him on the raised platform in front of the audience. Then we started:

Simon: "How are you feeling right now?"

Me: "I'm feeling fine."

Simon: "Bullshit, how are you really feeling?"

Me: Nervously laughing. "I'm feeling anxious."

Simon: "I'm feeling anxious because?"

Me: "I'm feeling anxious because strangers are watching, I've never done this before, and I don't know what I will find."

Simon: "I'm afraid of what I will find because?"

Me: "I'm afraid and anxious because they might see how sad I am."

Simon: "I'm sad because?"

Me: "I'm sad because I have not been in a relationship for quite some time and I am feeling very alone."

Simon: "I'm feeling alone because?"

Me: "I'm feeling alone because I've no one to share my life with."

Simon: "I need someone in my life because?"

Me: Crying now. "I need someone in my life because it makes me feel alive and accepted."

Simon: "What you are uncovering at this moment is that place in you that yearns for closeness with a woman, and when it isn't there you don't feel seen. I'm going to ask you to reflect and journal thoughts about growing up and your relationship with your mother. And in a non-blaming way, think about what was missing in this relationship. Then I want you to reflect on what would it be like for you if you didn't need to have someone in your life as a way to define yourself."

With that, Simon closed the session by smiling while looking at me profoundly, then hugging me. I noticed that I felt very exposed to the group, yet at the same time very quiet inside. I had indeed seen myself, and despite being reminded that I wasn't perfect, that was OK because I had just learned something powerful about myself. I was intrigued and eager to see where this new process for looking into myself would lead.

After two more people underwent brief "resourcing" sessions with Simon, Peggy Davenport, co-founder of SAGE and Bill's partner, came on stage and began to talk.

Peggy was a gorgeous, curly-haired blond woman who was younger than Bill, closer to my age. Her soft, clear voice echoed the smile on her round face. As Peggy talked, I felt a connection: She was describing aspects of my life. She explained having done work she didn't like and having felt stuck in her life. Peggy told us that at a particularly difficult time she'd been standing on a lanai in a Hawaiian hotel contemplating ending her life... when she met Bill. He had been on the patio below, looking up at her on the lanai, and somehow, he knew how unhappy she was and what she was contemplating. He kept waving at her to come down to the pool area. Peggy went on to say that seeing Bill wave made her realize she was not invisible. Wondering why this stranger was waving at her, she thought, what the heck, and went down to meet this man. When Bill spoke to her for the very first time, he told her he sensed her sadness but also saw her greatness, beauty, and light.

Peggy's honesty, sincerity, and humility, displayed right there in front of us, was beautiful, and it gave an authenticity to the gathering. I felt privileged to witness this open sharing from one human being to all of us sitting in the audience. At that moment, I wondered for the first time if it might be possible to have a job that earned income and enabled me to lead a life assisting others to live up to their potential.

Something had clicked in a deep place inside me. I sensed that SAGE might not be the best program for me to choose for incorporating new practices into my life, but still, it gave me my first look at a real opportunity to do just that.

Peggy's talk ended, and people associated with SAGE started circulating the room asking people privately if they would care to attend the upcoming corporate basic seminar in San Rafael, California, which is where I was temporarily living. I expected Josephine to come up to me and try to sign me up, but she didn't. As I turned to gather my stuff and leave, Peggy walked up and asked me what I thought. I complimented her on her willingness to be forthcoming about her story and said it had touched me. Then she asked, "What is your next step?" I smiled, knowing that I was being enrolled, and said, "I want to go the Dreamwalk seminar, and how much should I make the check out for?" She smiled and said, "$295.00." I handed her the check and said: "I'll see you in two weeks."

I walked over to Michael B. and asked if he had signed up for the upcoming seminar. He had. As we began talking about SAGE's business model and its underpinning, Bill Dempsey joined us. We continued our discussion, drawing Bill in with questions, and he said, "Why don't you guys drive up to Rohnert Park next week, and I'll answer all your questions then." We made an appointment. Michael B. and I exchanged phone numbers and set up a time to meet before we went to SAGE Headquarters. I didn't know then that Michael B. would become one of my SAGE partners.

Our meeting with Bill turned out to be long, confusing, yet informative. We learned that Bill had no written business plan and little documentation on SAGE's current status or processes, but that Peggy and Bill had an intense desire to bring something powerful and unique to the public. The SAGE founders had a real enthusiasm for what they were doing and believed in it.

As we began to pack up and leave, Bill challenged us by asking, "What are your next steps?"

Both of us answered his call to action the same way. We needed to think about what he had told us and consider our options before investing $10,000 each in this venture. Raising his voice, Bill began to berate us for wasting his time if we weren't going to step up and become part of SAGE.

"You both need to make the next step," he bellowed in a very challenging voice. After a pause, he raised his voice even higher and shouted, "Now tell me. What is your next step?"

Chapter 10

Bamboozled or Bamboo

I am not easily bullied or bamboozled, and I certainly wasn't willing to decide my involvement with SAGE before I had the information I wanted. My next step was to experience what SAGE was offering while tucking Bill's aggressive comments into the back of my mind. I knew that I would address all this later.

Just as I had bought and used the Tony Robbins "Personal Power" tapes and done a resourcing session with Simon, my next step with SAGE was to experience the content of their seminars to find out more about them. It wasn't appropriate for me to invest $10,000 in becoming a "Sage Master" and putting on personal growth seminars if I didn't learn and grow from these seminars myself. And for the moment, I certainly didn't think I was sufficiently trained to deliver them.

What had turned me off about the "Personal Power" tapes is they're based on a philosophy of changing myself from the outside. In other words, by reprogramming certain behaviors I'd change. Intuitively, this seemed more like a band-aid approach to change. And with most outside-in approaches, they don't last. Yes, I might have programmed my external actions and behaviors to get my previous job, but I wasn't necessarily happy, nor did it free me from my inner turmoil.

The concept of re-programming myself through Neuro-linguistic Programming (NLP), as Tony taught, seemed surface-oriented. As I'd learned from my biofeedback and behavior modification courses and research with Dr. Welgan at UCI, outward behavior can be changed and modified through behavioral programming, but deeply rooted feelings, values and belief systems are less effected. Human beings are deeper and more complicated than this, and to be deeply happy and internally free appeared would require more than a behavior change. Tony's basic thought seemed to say that I could re-program my current unsuccessful patterned responses to events into new, lasting, successful actions and be happy because of the results. This re-programming included visualizing the future in a way that I would see as successful and re-programming myself to live that prosperous future now. Tony also talked about needing to achieve "emotional mastery" and the need to master "the science of achievement" and "the art of fulfillment."

Tony's program sounded good. However, it gave me the impression of being shallow or simplistic (not saying it's easy) in that it pushed deeply rooted conflicts or unresolved wounds aside. To me, attempting to replace these pushed-aside wounds, conflicts, and issues with new behaviors weren't congruent with integrating change based on a grander more centered foundation.

What had driven me to the cliff's edge wasn't a series of things that could be reprogrammed. My intuition told me that facing, coming to grips with, understanding and resolving or accepting deeply rooted issues and inner wounds could result in a more permanent change and personal freedom. Although I think the "Personal Power" programs are effective at assisting people to be more outwardly successful, I don't believe they enhanced inner peace or true freedom.

My success wasn't going to be measured by the type of car I drove, a job title, or the amount of money in my bank account. What I wanted was to better recognize who I was, embrace this person by healing my wounds, and come from a more spiritually centered place. I wanted freedom from the sufferings that bound me.

With SAGE, my goal was to learn what it had to offer from both an experiential point of view and as a possible business venture by helping others. There would be little value in my investing in a developing a SAGE territory if I couldn't have the experience I'd want others to have. Learning from experience has always been what works best for me.

Despite my excitement about the possibility of becoming a personal growth seminar leader, it wasn't lost on me that, though I'd just been through a life-changing event, I was currently ill-prepared to teach people how to improve their lives. Just because I'd chosen to live instead of stepping off a cliff didn't mean I had any secrets to life. It indicated only that maybe I was ready to learn something. However, I did think the experience I had just gone through would help me relate to people who'd had difficult times. I also knew my willingness to dive in and work to change my life would be helpful in working with others.

I had signed up for the Dreamwalk seminar and knew that if I wanted to go through the whole training to become a Sage Master, I'd have to spend about $1,500 and about nine to twelve months' time taking their series of seminars and workshops to develop myself into a Dreamwalk seminar leader. The money for the seminars would be on top of the $10,000 to purchase a protected territory to deliver Dreamwalk seminars.

What I had hoped was: To learn about myself and to acquire the skills to teach the seminars. And determine if the SAGE organization was worthy of my investment of time and money.

I planned to take each of SAGE's three public seminars in succession and determine how effective they were and whether I'd recommend sending people from my Dreamwalk workshops to the following corporate workshops. This first one was put on by SAGE's corporate staff as an example of how a proper Dreamwalk seminar would work.

The 'Dreamwalk' Seminar

When I arrived, people were milling about and guided to the chairs in the front of the room. When those chairs filled, SAGE staff pulled chairs from the back and placed them behind the filled rows. All told there seemed to be about 60 people taking this seminar.

I detected accents from every corner of the United States and walking past small groups of people I caught the gist of some of their conservations. There were questions about what might happen during the seminar, discussion about the viability of SAGE's business model, and speculation about its Dreamwalk Seminar being merely a teaser for its other two corporate-hosted public workshops: 'Magic Maker' and 'Master Quest.' Other conversations focused on how Sage Masters would find enough people to willing to pay nearly $300 for a two-and-a-half-day personal growth seminar and whether it would be worthwhile.

After we were all settled into our seats, Josephine introduced Bill Dempsey. Bill kicked the day off with a short overview of SAGE. He stated that the primary objective of SAGE's public seminars was to give its attendees new ways to see, understand, and own up to their behaviors. Then, through this gained understanding, they would be equipped to make the behavioral changes they desired in their lives. SAGE believed that real change happens at a deep core level and that to get to this core, people needed to understand their current behavior and then to experience it with this new understanding.

This belief that change happens at a deep core place was just what I wanted to hear. And although I promised myself to use my discerning mind while taking these seminars, I thought we were off to a good start.

Bill went on to say that in SAGE the continuum of behavior-to-understanding consists of five levels. He illustrated them with a diagram: five concentric circles representing the five levels of behavior/understanding. The levels are Attitudes, Behaviors, Sub-Conscious Programs, Belief Systems, and Feelings and Values.

The following drawing is a visual representation of this diagram and these levels.

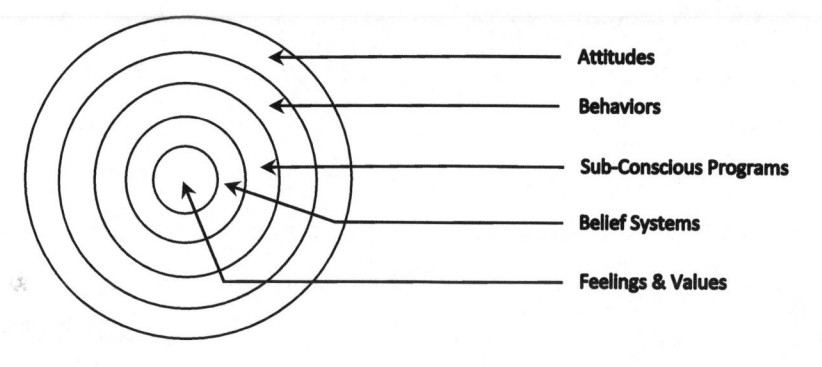

Attitudes

Behaviors

Sub-Conscious Programs

Belief Systems

Feelings & Values

Discovering our most profound truths at the level of Feelings and Values (in my case, that neither money nor relationships would bring me true and deep happiness) can create shifts at the core level of our being. These shifts, because they feel congruent with what is right for our soul and spirit, enduringly change our values and feelings. When we transform ourselves at this level, the change reverberates through all the other levels, resulting in new and different behavior (the outermost level). This behavior change can be subtle and barely recognizable, or it can be more overt.

During the "Dreamwalk" seminar, which was led by Bill D., Peggy D., and Simon W., we learned more about identifying our behaviors, how they manifested, and how to recognize our undesirable behaviors that stemmed from false beliefs, feelings, and values.

This seminar consisted of multiple segments. Depending on the complexity of the section, each one could take up to two or more hours to complete. Each part was introduced with a topic statement about the particular subject it would cover, such as 'truthfulness,' which was followed by a "set-up" discussion, then a break, and finally the experiential exercise that aimed at discovery.

The set-ups, approximately 45 minutes to an hour in length, consisted of one or more speakers sharing a personal story related to the topic and telling us what they have learned about that subject. The set-ups while liberally sprinkled with either famous or not well-known, quotes always shed light on an aspect of the subject matter.

Once the set-up was complete, our leaders gave us a 15-to-30-minute break, usually with instructions on what to do during the break. For instance, on the second day, one topic we addressed was forgiveness. During the break, we had to come up with something we did or said that did wasn't in alignment with our integrity – something of which being forgiven would be a relief or uplifting. Therefore, our goal was to dig deep into our lives and find something that we may have buried a long time ago. We were to share this "unspoken secret" with our "dyad partner" (a fellow participant who serves as our partner during the seminar), include a bit of the background of this deed, and do this with complete confidence that the information shared would not be expressed to anyone else—ever.

My dyad partner was a man I will call Bob. Bob was huge. Standing next to him might have been intimidating, but there was a reassuring sweet softness about him. After agreeing to the statement of confidentiality, I sat across from Bob and shared one of my forbidden secrets. The act of telling this very intimate story with another person brought up feelings of sadness, sorrow, embarrassment, and new thoughts on the event.

After listening to the story, Bob just said: "Michael, you are forgiven for everything you ever thought, felt, said, or done, and it is so." I replied with "Thank you," and then we switched roles.

No one assumed that just one experience during the seminar would significantly change his or her behavior or understanding. The goal was to shine a light on a previously hidden set of feelings or values. With this goal achieved, and with additional practice and more time, the transformation would be possible.

The power of this straightforward exercise brought home the potential of this seminar if one was willing to open up to look deeper. Trust was vital because one had to be ready to go out on a limb and trust another human being with a secret. Just as I had learned in the dyad with Simon, the actual, out-loud sharing was an enormously powerful and effective way to free oneself of remorse, and for me in this sharing, shame.

We had numerous other set-ups and exercises during this two-and-a-half-day seminar. Some of them involved discovering where our anger comes from; others pushed into the area of what we wished for as a child. Additionally, we worked on our life success plans, during which we used pictures cut out from magazines, glued to a 2' x 3' white poster board, to helped us to visualize how we wanted our life to be. For example, if we were looking for serenity, we would use pictures that we felt depicted this state of mind.

When the Dreamwalk Seminar ended, I reflected on what I had learned and concluded that it had been worthwhile. Although my SAGE experience, thus far, was that the staff could be pushy and possibly not entirely aboveboard, the exercises during this seminar had challenged my values and patterns of behavior and opened me to new modes of thought. For better or for worse, I decided to take the next public SAGE course called Magic Maker, after attending their non-public Sage Master 'Candidate Training' course.

The Candidate Training was designed to assist Bill and Peggy in determining if a candidate would be a good Sage Master as they observed the candidate's engagement and abilities to work in groups, lead groups, and present information. It put us through various types of experiential exercises that trained us to lead groups through conceptual ideas and dialogue.

One of the priorities we discussed during the Candidate Training was to be present with oneself as well as with each candidate. The ability to be in the here and now with yourself would be critically important when delivering seminars. Although Candidate Training wasn't as experientially based as the Dreamwalk or the upcoming Magic Maker, I derived essential insights about myself that would stay with me.

One of the more powerful pieces of wisdom I gained from the candidate training was encapsulated in a quote that Bill shared: "Fascination is the bridge between fear and love." He meant that we could limit fear-based thought by looking at the unknown with fascination instead of fear. Such an enlightened approach to fear inspired me to consider the nature of fear itself. Fear of physical danger is undoubtedly real and vital to my survival. But if I create fear from the inside, then it could become a type of fear called a **F**alse **E**xperience **A**ppearing **R**eal.

Mark Twain had a wonderful saying for what our minds can create and conjure up while in a state of fear: "I am an old man and have known a great many troubles, but most of them never happened." Fear does this. It creates thoughts and feelings that are often not based on truth or the reality of the moment.

I knew from personal experience about inventing reasons to be afraid. At the time of this seminar, I still had an acute fear of heights. This fear would show up at different times and places. For example, in my previous job I had to fly a lot. My apprehension about flying got to the point where I would need a couple of Scotches on the rocks before getting on the plane, and even then, all my airplane trips were white-knuckle flights. My worst fear was that the pilot was going to hit something, especially during landings, and there was nothing I could do about it.

Another episode brought on by my fear of heights took place at a Neil Young with Crazy Horse concert at the Dorothy Chandler Pavilion in Los Angeles in November 1976. I was sitting in the second row of the balcony and kept thinking that I would fall over the balcony railing and die. Neil Young happens to be my favorite singer-songwriter and feeling that I was going to die at any moment by dropping from the balcony put a damper, to say the least, on my enjoyment of the concert.

My phobia kicked in with horrifying intensity on another occasion, this time in July 1987. I was standing on the observer's deck of the Seattle Space Needle and became frozen with fear that a supreme burst of wind was going to lift me and toss me over the side railing, plummeting me to my death. Another potentially wonderful experience ruined by "False Experience Appearing Real."

These fears of mine were self-created, and at the time, I had no discernable ability to see past them.

Specifically, the "False Experience Appearing Real" in my head was my perception that I was going to die in some very freakish accident. The actual likelihood of this happening was extremely remote. Plane crashes were rare. The balcony railing at the Dorothy Chandler Pavilion is at least 42 inches high, and my seat was nearly 10 feet away from the barrier. The amount of wind needed to lift me over the barrier at the top of the Space Needle would have to be stupendous; besides, a six-year-old girl standing in front of me at the railing enjoyed the view in complete safety and without fear.

Now, this doesn't mean that having fears isn't at times useful. When we were cave dwellers and hunters and gatherers, fear tuned us into the dangers lurking behind a rock, bush, or tree. We needed a way to pump adrenaline immediately into our bloodstream and take flight or fight our way through the danger. Even today, fear mobilizes us to make quick choices when we need them. What this SAGE candidate training taught me was that many of my fears were irrational, such as my fear of heights, and it inspired me to conquer these fears.

The 'Magic Maker' Seminar

The Magic Maker seminar was the second of SAGE's three public seminars. It was a four-day workshop billed as an advanced seminar for graduates of the Dreamwalk led by the Bill and Peggy and their senior trainers. This seminar was held in Rohnert Park. There were nearly 50 participants, which surprised me because only about 20 of them were graduates of the Dreamwalk seminar I had attended. The rest, I discovered, were graduates of other Dreamwalk seminars that were either SAGE corporate-sponsored or from seminars sponsored by Sage Masters. Having these attendees was proof that Bill and Peggy's model was working.

The first order of business was to begin opening to our deeper selves. To that end, we did a series of Kundalini meditations under the guidance of Larry J., who was a senior SAGE instructor. Larry was also a co-founder of LifeSpring, Alpha Mind Dynamics, and creator of the meditative Psychogenesis process. Larry had an impressive look about him. His golden tan was illuminated by long white hair flowing just past his shoulders, accentuating his white Van Dyke beard. Dressed smartly in silk shirts and loose-fitting whitish gauze pants, he looked the part of a wise master.

Although I'd never done Kundalini meditations before this, I'd heard that they were powerful, energetic meditations that primarily focused on aligning and engaging the body's chakra energy from its base through the head. Everyone experiences a Kundalini mediation differently, but an excellent descriptive picture might be to say it is like a coiled snake rising through the spine and out the head in a blissful way.

These energies, Larry explained, would start from the Muladhara or root chakra located at the base of the spine in the coccygeal region of the body and move up in a swirling pattern to the Sahasrara or crown chakra located at the top of the head. As we got deeper into the initial one-hour meditation, my body seemed to start swirling, and I felt a surge of power that could only be this Kundalini energy spinning wildly within me. It was both exhilarating and exhausting.

In this seminar, we followed a powerful Kundalini meditation with an investigation into our family's pasts lives to learn more about how our generational family may guide our behaviors and personalities. First, we created a "genogram," a graphic representation of the personalities and interplay of our family's generations.

Larry had us construct a "genogram," listing descriptive words that my close relatives used to describe family members I'd not met or who had passed on, and I began to see patterns of behavior in my family, especially in my parents.

Catchphrases that my parents and my fraternal grandmother often used to describe their direct family, relatives, and themselves included "salt of the earth," "nose to the grindstone," "tough as nails," "workaholic," "toes the line," "driven," and "hard worker." Reviewing this listing of family descriptors, it came home to me that being raised with these values and that they, in turn, were formed over generations in response to historical forces. Spotlighting the phrases and how they could influce behavior began to shine a light on why my parents made the choices they did while raising me.

In the light of these realizations, I found a deeper understanding of my childhood. Not only did I receive only one bike, but I recall receiving homemade wooden rifles to play with outside. Whereas other kids got store-bought rifles, my dad made us toy rifles out of scrap wood from his garage workshop. He was very skilled and made them look great. He also refurbished his childhood train set, and I recall getting up one Christmas morning to find the train running on the floor in the living room with him at the controls, a boyish grin on his face.

My parents put a lot of effort into these gifts for me. The presents were a sign that we didn't have much money and even as a child I often felt as though there was tension in our home due to our meager finances. I appreciated their efforts to always have food on the table, a warm bed at night, and clothes on our backs, but these efforts also created difficulties. I was expected to be a representative of the family, and when my behavior didn't meet their expectations, I was punished. The punishment came verbally through yelling, being told I was terrible, and sometimes physically by being his with a hand, or a leather belt that would break the skin. The pain of being hit like this led me to be very guarded about expressing my feelings.

Being sensitive to their reactions and behavior towards me, I hid and often lied to keep what I felt was my safety net.

After the genogram, Simon W. offered to do a "resourcing" session in front of the group. Because I'd gotten so much out of the genogram work and my previous meeting with Simon, I volunteered to do the resourcing dialogue with him and was not disappointed.

Simon: "How are you feeling right now?"

Me: "I'm feeling anxious."

Simon: "I'm feeling anxious because…"

Me: "I'm feeling anxious because I don't know what is going to happen in front of everyone here."

Simon: "I'm afraid of what is going to happen to me because…"

Me: "I'm afraid of this welling up of feelings and emotions that are building up inside of me. I don't know what's happening."

Simon: "I'm afraid of letting go of my feelings because…"

Me: (Bursting out in tears and not being able to contain myself with any control, I mumbled) "I don't want to be here. I don't know why I was born. I wasn't welcomed and felt tricked into coming to this earth. How come there is no love here?"

Simon: (Reaching out putting his hand gently on my shoulder) "I know it hurts when you don't feel that you belong here."

Sitting there in front of all those people, I felt a massive movement of energy coming through me in waves. My face became contorted with the painful internal memory as tears just flowed, and my body convulsed with angst. Coming out of this pain, I could see the empathy from the group. That felt nice, but I also felt embarrassment from exposing myself so profoundly and emotionally in front of them.

My life to that point, I realized, was not congruent with my imaginings of what I thought my life would be like, and I'm sure I share this experience with many others. Often, childhood experiences are responsible for these sensations of feeling out of sorts and incongruent with the world around us and our perceptions of what the world is supposed to be. I do think our parents do their best to raise us, but how they raised us is often a deep reflection of how they were reared. Therefore, our interactions with our parents may not supply us with what we believe we need.

By saying this, I am not condoning behaviors exhibited by parents. Acceptance does not mean condoning. Acceptance only means that one sees what is, with empathy and without judgment.

Several more exercises invited us to experience some of our deep-rooted feelings about our upbringing and the belief structures we inherited while growing up. Two of the activities aimed directly at our relationship with, and perceptions of, our parents.

One of these two exercises included meditation and process called psychogenesis—a term for the origin and development of psychological processes and their resulting behavior. It contrasts with one's physiological development. The object of our psychogenesis meditation was to be guided back through our lives as far back as possible, even to before our birth, and note events as they transpired and how we felt, responded and reacted to these events. Additionally, as we were guided back to the current moment, we were to pay particular attention to how those events manifested in current behavior. The exercise provided a glimpse of myself coming into this world and sensing that it didn't seem to be what I expected to experience. I had been looking to be loved, nurtured, and seen. My experience was something different.

Rounding out these powerful exercises was a session on forgiveness. I was already learning that forgiveness was a potent healing tool. In this segment, the men stood next to each other facing inward in a half circle, and the women positioned together completing the ring so that there was one big circle with men making up one half and women the other half. One of the men standing next to a woman was asked to start by moving into the circle and facing the man who had been standing next to him. The man on the inside gently took the hands of the man on the outside of the circle and said: "I forgive you, Dad, I forgive you, Dad, I forgive you, Dad." The person standing on the outside being addressed responded with "Thank you." As the person on the inside moved to the next person (a man) standing on the outside, the inside person again said: "I forgive you, Dad, I forgive you, Dad, I forgive you, Dad." And again, the man standing on the outside who was being addressed responded with "Thank you." As the initial man moved to the next person, the second man moved to the inside of the circle and stood in front of and held the hands of the person on the outside. The same "I forgive you, Dad" and "Thank you" statements were made by each of the inside and outside person respectively. The peeling-off of each person from the outside to the inside was continuous. As the men began to stand in front of the women, the statement for the inside person changed to: "I forgive you, Mom, I forgive you, Mom, I forgive you, Mom." Again, the person standing on the outside being addressed responded with "Thank you."

Once the first man had finished addressing all the men and woman in the circle, he turned around and stood on the outside facing in and became the recipient of the "I forgive you ..." line and responded with "Thank you." This smooth rotation and process continued until all the men and women interacted with everyone else on both sides of the dialogue.

My first experience of addressing the men was relatively easy. However, I also noticed that the feeling behind my words wasn't intense. When I reached the first woman, I froze. I couldn't get the words "I forgive you" out of my mouth. I was flush with anger and hurt. I felt powerful resistance to forgiving my mother for all the many things I think she needed to do to welcome me, hold me, and embrace me into this world. As I had just discovered through the psychogenesis meditation, I was struggling with being in this world, and her dis-attachment with me had amplified my not wanting to be here.

At long last, I was able to bring myself to express forgiveness to the first woman in the line. Moving to each woman, I could see her caring and feel her empathy for me in her specific and personal way. I started to see the unique person in the eyes of each woman I faced. I saw the different ways each of them cared and how the caring is expressed differently. Reflecting on this, I began to see versions of my mother in each of these women. Emotions and tears flowed as feelings of true of caring and forgiveness poured forth.

Once everyone had completed one cycle of the circle, we all stood in silence, except for the sniffling and the sounds of people audibly crying. We all held hands spontaneously. After about 10 minutes, we were instructed to go through the same process again. This time, when it came to my turn to move to the inside, I noticed I immediately paid more attention and opened myself to a deeper level of forgiveness to both the men and women. It was powerfully cathartic.

Later in the Magic Maker training, the SAGE instructor was Mark S., who was a 10th Degree Black Belt and Shodan Ninjutsu Master. Mark is Asian with intense yet kind eyes. His manner of movement steeped in a learned practice. His air of authority and clarity in speaking made him an excellent teacher.

Mark worked both in the martial and healing arts. Besides being a Black Belt, he trained in the Hawaiian healing art of Ho'oponopono – "to make right" or "to rectify an error." His forte was to combine these two disciplines' seemingly opposed principles into a single spiritual teaching.

During one of our sessions with Mark, the group performed a couple of powerful exercises that addressed how we approached the wishes and challenges in our lives. Per SAGE, we often allow our fear of success or failure to create roadblocks to completing tasks. We had previously covered ground about our feelings and values and how they construct belief systems that can constrict us. With Mark as our guide, we began to explore past times during in which we limited ourselves by not having a clear intention. We completed two different exercises that focused on our intentions and limits. The first exercise involved breaking boards with our hands in two ways: One way was with mighty force and purpose, using our strength to fracture the wood board. The second way was designed to have us better understand that we can split the same kind of wood board just as effectively with quiet, soft, but clear intention. When we employed the first way, we shouted out a loud noise as we drove our hand down on the board. When we used the second way, we pushed our hand through the wood plank without making any noise. This demonstration drove home to me the power of having a clear intention. The second exercise on intention impacted me even more profoundly. It was called The Bamboo Party.

I had first seen the Bamboo Party demonstrated at the Candidate Training course, three weeks earlier. The episode had been jaw-dropping and difficult for me to watch, and I thought there was only a minimal chance that I would ever participate in such a thing. The Bamboo Party struck me as too dangerous and extreme to be appropriate for a human-growth workshop. Nevertheless, I had come to respect Mark S., so I was open to considering it, though reluctantly.

According to Mark, the Bamboo Party was one of the steps to becoming a Shodan Ninjutsu Master. It is part of the initiation process and consisted of three levels: One Bamboo, Three Bamboo, and Five Bamboo.

The exercise was volunteer-only because of its intensity and became a compelling example of intention. In light that I had promised myself on this journey towards personal freedom and happiness that I would be willing to do almost anything, and since I'd seen someone survive the One Bamboo Party, I was ready to give it a go.

Mark instructed me to lie down on the floor of the room with my hands at my sides. The other participants gathered in a semicircle about 10 feet from my feet.

Kneeling on each side of my head were two strong men; Mark stood above my head as a guide.

In Mark's hand was a five-foot-long pole of bamboo approximately two inches in diameter. Mark explained that upon my signal, the two men would lay the bamboo across my neck and press it down so that the ends of the pole touched the floor. The men committed to holding their ends of the bamboo on the floor, across my neck, and not letting them up unless Mark told them to do so. Because the bamboo was so thick, I knew that it wasn't going to bend much, if at all, when pressed across my neck. It would probably cause a near collapse of my windpipe, obviously hindering breathing and hurting like hell.

The goal was to escape from under the bamboo pole without using my hands. "You either get out or pass out," Mark told us in an ominous and serious tone of voice. Speaking clearly and quietly, he assured us that the bamboo exercise is offered on a volunteer basis only in the Magic Maker workshops. "This exercise is about intention and finding the place within us that drives us to do powerful things." As Mark shared this information, a fearful silence descended on the group.

The volunteers grasped their ends of the bamboo and positioned themselves to push the ends to the floor upon my command. I recall Mark asking me if I was ready, and I heard myself say, "Yes." For some reason, I cannot fathom why, I felt relaxed and centered, so I raised my right hand, dropped it and slapped the floor, and before I knew it everything went into an adrenalin panic mode.

The bamboo across my neck was suddenly choking me. I couldn't breathe. Every slight movement of my head created more agony and more panic. Painfully, I turned my head and felt small relief as I could now, cripplingly, suck in a little air. I felt trapped, and the pressure of the bamboo was painful, but I felt a flash of reassurance because the pain seemed to have stabilized. I attempted to move my head out from underneath the bamboo. I could feel the hard scraping against my temple and forehead. My ear was folded over, and I knew it was damaged. Then, as if I had gone unconscious, with a sudden burst of energy coming from the center of my body, my will to live leading the way, I saw myself standing up looking down at the bamboo. I felt wild and filled with adrenaline-fueled power. It was over, and I heard some applause from the people watching. I was filled with hyper energy.

I attempted to take in my thoughts and feelings. It was difficult to calm down, so I went outside for a short walk. The fresh air immediately felt invigorating and brought me to a more centered place, while a few deep breaths reduced my pent-up energy and adrenaline to a manageable level. I found a nearby restroom and went to the sink. Looking up at my face in the mirror, I turned on the faucet as I viewed the cuts on my forehead and behind the flap of my left ear. I bent down over the sink, and I splashed water on my face. The fresh water brought an increased awareness of where I was and what I had just experienced. I inhaled a deep breath and smiled. What would be next?

When I walked back into the room, another volunteer was about to attempt to free himself from the bamboo across his neck. Peggy walked over and quietly whispered into my ear, "Journal your thoughts."

My journal reads: "I can find the determination to overcome any fear I may have. I do want to live. I will live. 'Love is the opening door; love is what we came here for, no one could offer you more. Do you know what I mean? Have your eyes really seen?'" (The last part comes from an Elton John song.)

Chapter 11

Fearless Presence

On my path to becoming a Sage Master, I had to gain additional knowledge about producing and leading SAGE Dreamwalk seminars. Supporting the transition to become a Sage Master, prospects were required to serve as staff at SAGE seminars. To this end, I signed up to help as a staff member during the New York City Dreamwalk and Magic Maker seminars.

At this point, I'd completed Dreamwalk, Magic Maker, and the Candidate Training seminars, but had yet to sign a Sage Master agreement. Before signing the contract and paying the fee, I needed to resolve a couple of issues with Bill about the way he ran the organization and gain enough confidence that I could effectively deliver Dreamwalk seminars.

One obstacle was my unsettled skepticism about SAGE's business practices. Although my due diligence—speaking with a couple of Sage Masters who were successfully delivering Dreamwalk seminars—gave me reasons to join the Sage team, these Sage Masters also had a few of the same questions I did about Bill's business integrity.

My second issue was not knowing if I had it in me to become a successful staffer and deliverer of Dreamwalk seminars. It appeared that Bill believed that by taking all the public courses along with the Candidate Training, Warrior Path seminar, and the Instructor Training, one would be prepared to deliver Dreamwalk seminars.

On one level, I saw that this could be useful because the exercises in Dreamwalk weren't very specialized, advanced, or potentially dangerous like the Bamboo Party. I was asking myself, "Is it enough and are the people going through the Sage Master training people I'd want to be led by?" I wasn't sure yet.

Since I'd already taken the Candidate Training course for potential Sage Masters, I now had my chance to test my potential as a SAGE leader. I traveled to New York City on my dime to be part of the staff for a set of Dreamwalk, Candidate Training, and Magic Maker workshops.

During the process of putting these workshops together, I'd spoken with several SAGE participants who had responded to the same sort of ad that I had. Like me, these people were interested in consciously growing from the inside out, which was exciting for me to hear, and they were potential Sage Masters as well. Working with fellow future Sage Masters, in these workshops, helped to make our connection exciting and based in solidarity of our challenges.

During the New York City Dreamwalk seminar, I got my first taste of working as a team with other new staff members to deliver the best possible training for the attendees. In this seminar, there was an exercise called "Yes/No." It involved lying on your back while an instructor provided specific visualizations. After being guided through visualization, the participants would loudly shout out "yes" or "no" repeatedly depending on the type of visualization.

As members of the staff, our role was to support the attendees through this experience. After the instructor guided the participants through a particularly powerful visualization based on forgiveness, participants were instructed to shout "no" from deep within themselves for about two minutes. The energy emanating from 78 screaming people lying on their backs was potent.

I happened to be standing next to a man who jumped up about 90 seconds into his "no's." Turning quickly, he spied me, grabbed me in a full bear hug, and started crying. His body heaved as he sobbed uncontrollably in my arms. I gently held him as he calmed down, and after about three minutes, we stepped outside the room where he told me how hard it had been for him to forgive himself for killing people during his many bombing missions over Vietnam.

He didn't know I was the only person on the SAGE staff who had fought in Vietnam and had myself done a lot of forgiveness work around taking a life. There are no coincidences.

This experience was heartening because, once again, my experience and willingness to show up to myself and to be in the present supported my belief that I was not only learning more about myself but also gaining the ability to share my compassionate and empathetic self.

With a short break between my job of staffing the Dreamwalk and Magic Maker seminars and feeling emboldened by my recent success of a Three Bamboo Party and other experiences, I could not wait to take my new stronger spirit for a test drive. And the perfect FEAR dragon for me to slay was right there in New York City.

As I've said, I have a fear of heights. I don't recall what age I was when I first encountered this phobia. What I do know is that over the last 15 years, this fear had become unbearable. It severely affected my ability to enjoy various events and attractions. It made my four-times-a-week airplane flights in the mid-1980s extremely difficult. It kept me from going to the top of the Eiffel Tower when I visited Paris and, as I've said, it made trips to places such as the top of the Space Needle in Seattle extremely uncomfortable. It was an irrational FEAR, and now I was going to use the power of my better understanding of fear gained in these past few months to challenge my phobia by going to the top of the Empire State Building. I specifically chose this building because when I was growing up, it was the tallest building in the world. Today, I know, there are other taller buildings, but to me, the Empire State Building still held this title.

Stepping outside the hotel, I got into a taxi and told the driver, "Take me to the Empire State Building." Looking up at the skyscraper's 102 stories, it came home to me how much the inner work I'd done over the last few months had changed me. With my new-found power, I stood in front of the mammoth base of this towering spire, and said, "Today, I will conquer you. I will conquer myself."

The first elevator ride was terrific. I was still riding on the momentum of my newfound power. But when I got off the elevator and realized I was only part way up and had to take another one to the top, I started to feel the buildup of anxiety that was always the precursor to my fear of heights.

I got on the second elevator, and the old FEAR started roaring back despite my efforts to reason with myself that I needed to be in the here and now and not to succumb to this "false experience." Swallowing my nerves, I got into this very far-above-the-ground elevator and closed my eyes as I felt the upward "whoop." When I opened them, there in the elevator with me was a young girl who also appeared to be very afraid. I fully identified with her visible expression of fear, which intensified my own arising concerns and kicked off a good dose of panicked based perspiration.

When the doors opened, I managed to exit, but only by looking down at the cement below my feet rather than in the direction of the dreaded space somewhere in front of me. Slowly I walked out onto the observation deck, and slowly I lifted my eyes to see the vastness of New York. The brisk wind briskly hit my face. Again, I closed my eyes, this time to brace myself by breathing in a slow, steady rhythm. I recalled my proclaimed intention and got to work grounding myself by telling myself what was real. The reality was that I was standing near the very pinnacle of a building that had stood there for well over 50 years, making my fear a "false experience appearing real" and that the likelihood of a strong wind lifting me up and over the railing or blowing the building over and killing me was specifically a "FEAR." Equally "false" was the notion that somehow, I was going to fall over the 12-foot-high barrier to my death. Opening my eyes and staying with my breathing, I gazed out at the fantastic New York skyline and the Hudson River and was struck by how beautiful the view was. Gingerly, I made my way around the observation deck I until I found the side that points more towards the lower end of Manhattan. I walked up to the barrier and looked down.

Immediately, I felt a hollowing out in my solar plexus, an open sunken sense of doom that always triggered the deep-rooted fear. Closing my eyes, I recalled my intention and focused on the rise and fall of my chest until I felt it move in a slower rhythm. I tried opening my eyes again and looked down. This time, there was the sensation of wonder and fascination. My heart opened, my stomach relaxed, and a smile began creeping across my face. Tension flowed from my hands and feet, while my breathing became quiet and natural. Suddenly I was experiencing joy, the joy of standing side-by-side with my intention and the extreme pleasure of seeing such an incredible view.

I taxied back to the hotel where the SAGE training was taking place on a wave of delight. I had stood on the iconic pinnacle of earth-defying height and shed my phobia. I embarked on the last phase of my training with a new certainty about my direction.

Back at the SAGE training, I entered the next phase of my training, presenting a workshop topic and tee-up as a SAGE staff member for Magic Maker, which was the precursor to the final graduate course, Master Quest. By now, being groomed for a leadership role as a Sage Master, and accordingly, I was assigned to be a presenter and to give a tee-up talk for a FEAR workshop.

For the FEAR assignment, I had prepared a couple of outlines that focused on my time in Vietnam. At the last minute, I decided to switch to an extemporaneous talk on my Empire State Building experience.

Although I was terrified of singing in my teenage rock band, I'd always been able to speak in front of others. I'd been on the speech and debate team in college, and impromptu speeches had been my favorite competitions. Calling on this background, I spoke about my past fear of heights and how challenging it had been to conquer it. As I spoke, I could see the audience connecting with my talk with head nods, knowing looks, and apparent interest. I told the story of my willingness to participate in the Three Bamboo Party, which many of the audience had witnessed, and how I'd used the technique of zeroing in with clear quiet intent to almost effortlessly moved out from under the three bamboo sticks. Lastly, I shared my experience of going to the top of the Empire State Building and reaching a level of awe and comfort at being at the top of this very tall building.

The group responded with a beautiful round of applause. Later during the break, it felt rewarding to receive many compliments and questions, which added weight to my dream of reaching out and connecting with people at a deep level.

Staffing these seminars had given me incredible confidence that I was on a positive path of change. And now I was ready to take the last course SAGE seminar, the graduate course called 'Master Quest.'

'Master Quest'

By now, I'd taken the Dreamwalk, Candidate Training, Magic Maker and Warrior Training seminars. In my capacity as an instructor in training, I also served as a staff member for the first three. My Instructor Training was nearly complete.

Although I hadn't fully committed to becoming a Sage Master, I was feeling very positive about what I had learned in the past seven months. Just as I had found a new-found strength in the seminars and workshops, I believed anyone who committed to doing the work required in them would gain knowledge and understanding about themselves.

My lingering questions about the SAGE infrastructure and territory contract would resolve themselves after Master Quest because that was my intention.

Master Quest was being held in Sedona, Arizona. I had only driven through Sedona and never spent time there, so I was looking forward to the experience.

The themes of Master Quest were the integration of oneself with everything else, the power of truth and spiritual connectedness and our innate ability to learn, love, be strong, and at peace. Many of these qualities, previously explored during the earlier seminars and workshops, led the SAGE leaders to believed that Sedona—which many people see as a hub of spiritual energies—was an ideal place for these concepts to come together.

So far, my personal growth from my SAGE experiences came from taking risks and opening to the opportunities that unfolded before me. I had been willing to take these risks because of the promise I made to myself that day standing on the cliff. Not taking risks would mean that I might be seeing opportunities for change as threats. I was learning that I tended to treat those threats in two counterproductive ways: By either attacking the danger verbally or physically or by avoiding the danger. Avoidance responses include running away, spacing out, getting sick, acting crazy, acting confused, using drugs or alcohol, wanting to sleep more than usual, or suicide.

One remedy for these pitfalls, I was learning, was to adopt a mentality of abundance rather than scarcity. Abundance fosters feelings of joy, ecstasy, fulfillment, happiness, and gratitude. When I approach life with a mindset of richness, I am more easily able to love, embrace peace, heal others, and find personal fulfillment. The Dalai Lama said: "Happiness is not something readymade. It comes from your own actions."

Scarcity, on the other hand, leads to disappointment, frustration, and anger. When living in the realm of scarcity, one can be fearful, hateful, possessive, and have a longing for security or safety. Helen Keller once said: "Safety and security is mostly a superstition. It does not exist in nature, nor do the children of men as a whole experience it. Avoiding danger is no safer in the long run than outright exposure. Life is either a daring adventure or nothing."

Candidly, nature lives in a realm where safety does not exist. Life, at this level, is the same for all sentient beings. It is always a risk. In that spirit, I walked into this workshop resolved to be open to all possibilities.

Along with Kundalini, Vipassana (the focus of which is insight), and guided visualization meditations, Master Quest introduced me to doing a form of concentration meditations called "sunset meditations." In these, we faced the setting sun every evening and focused our gaze at the sun. Each meditation was in a different location around Sedona. The most amazing of these meditations took place at a small airfield in Sedona. Here we would meditate at sunset gazing at the sun while in being in an "energy vortex." Larry told us that there were two types of energy vortexes, a male energy vortex, which puts a person (of either sex) in touch with how they value themselves, and a female energy vortex, which connects a person with the value he or she puts on others.

When our group arrived at the airfield, a male energy vortex, we began our meditation by standing in a circle holding hands. The sun was about an hour from hitting the horizon, and the warmth of the late afternoon wind filled us with a relaxed and peaceful feeling. My thoughts meandered back to the morning that day when we had made masks of our faces by dipping a waxy mesh material in hot water and placing it on our faces, gently pushing it around the contours. It felt oddly impactful to look in a mirror and see my face through a transparent mask.

Looking at the sun as it crept towards the distant horizon, we were instructed to reach out a hand toward it. I extended three fingers of my right hand in front of me so that the bottom finger lay on the upper edge of the distant horizon line and the top finger edged the bottom of the sun. "Another 15 minutes," I said to myself.

Our leaders had told us that when the sun reached the top edge of the index finger with the bottom side of the ring finger on the horizon line, it would be safe to look directly at the sun.

I rechecked the distance. It was just about time to begin. I closed my eyes and centered myself into deeper inner space, then opened them and stared directly into the light of the sun, letting all my thoughts go. Slowly, my body dissipated to the point where I had very little awareness of it, and my mind opened. I felt my crown chakra release the energy of the light connecting me to the vortex. My heart reached out through my eyes to touch the sun.

"I am of this light" was my first thought, and tears start flowing down my cheeks as an upwelling of joy rose from the center of my body and out through the top of my head.

I watched the sun until its lower edge touched the horizon, wanting this joy to last forever. Suddenly I understood that the sun would disappear, the same as all things, and that sweet, sad truth struck me with even more profound joy. As the sun touched the horizon, the soft sounds of a flute floated across the land around me. These are Indian melodies, I said to myself. A Native American perched on the hill behind me was playing the flute. The sounds danced across the flat top of a mesa shimmering in the distance and echoed off a closer mesa on my left. The magical and surreal notes reflected my feeling.

The last tiny edge of the sun disappeared, cooling the air, and the final long note from the flute ended. I closed my eyes in the silence, not daring to move and interrupt the serenity of the moment. Three or four minutes later, I sensed some movement and some gentle talking over my right shoulder. I ignored the distraction, opened my eyes, and gazed straight ahead because in front of me was a cliff edge just 20 feet away. I began making my way to the threshold of the cliff, this time not in despair but gratitude, spread my arms wide and opened my hands to feel the gently uplifting breeze coming from the distant valley floor below. As the wind swept across my outstretched arms, I leaned into it and felt lifted off the ground. I felt like an eagle soaring along the top edge of the cliff. I'd become part of the landscape as well as an entity in the scene.

I lifted one leg behind me and leaned even farther into the wind coming up through the valley floor and over the cliff edge. I was no longer afraid. I was soaring. I stayed that way until the wind began to subside. Then I lowered my arms to my sides. "I am of freedom," I thought with a smile.

And, as I had in a previous time, I moved away slowly from the cliff's edge. Back then it was because I was choosing life and this time it was more that I'd found life. I noticed a flat area nearby where I went and sat down for a moment. Then lying down, I looked at the sky as its color changed from light blue to a darker blue—Don Juan's crack in the universe, I thought.

Fascinated by the color of light and the clouds, I saw a cloud that mimicked my wax mesh mask, and I caught myself thinking: "You are light. You are love." And then "You are part of the whole." Consciously, I said aloud to myself: "I'm made of the light of the universe. I am part of the spirit of the universe. The spirit is part of me, and I am spirit."

For the second time in my lifetime, I momentarily felt as though I was part of the whole of everything and everyone. The first was the "Aum" meditation at a love-in. This time I was of the entire human race and the great spirit of the universe. I was the combination of these all of this, love and life.

The Medicine Wheel

At 6:30 AM the following morning, we gathered in the hotel parking lot to hop into vans and be taken on another spiritual journey, this time to a trailhead for an all-day hike into Indian Reservation land. Our destination was a Native American medicine wheel somewhere deep in one of the canyons. I had no idea that this little hike was going to disclose new humbling self-revelations.

At the trailhead parking lot, we hooked up with the partners we'd chosen at the beginning of the workshop. There were 36 of us in all, 18 sets of partners. My partner was named John. He was a banker from the east coast who, like myself, had grown tired of the rat race and get-what-you-can-before-anyone-else lifestyle. His well-manicured style and affluence were evident. At the same time, focused on expanding and changing his life and lifestyle.

Our instructions were direct. We'd be entering sacred land through an entrance marked by a set of piled stones about two feet high and about five feet apart, with the trail running between them. The second set of stones marked the path about 100 yards farther down the trail. At each of these points, we were to make a sacred offering of cornmeal that we were to lay on each pile of stones to honor the native cultures. Each time we placed the cornmeal on the rocks, we were to say our names and ask for permission to move past the stones. Mark S. was going to be standing at the second set of rocks and would say a prayer while we were offering the cornmeal. This way, we fully acknowledged our commitment to walk into this land with reverence, as if we were walking into a church.

This Magic Maker training began in earnest after making our offering at the second set of stones. There, we began a test of trust that also challenged our non-visual senses. Each member of the group wrapped a blindfold across a partner's eyes. I placed a blindfold over John's, eyes and he grasped my left elbow with his right hand as instructed. Each set of partners walked the trail like this, the blindfolded partner relying on the guiding partner and their remaining senses. The guides were to limit the use of their voices as much as possible.

Mark's instructions continued. As guides, our job was to keep our blindfolded partners out of trouble and safe. We had to be aware of keeping them in the middle of the trail, warning them off rocks, steps up, steps down, bushes, cliffs, and cliff walls. About every quarter mile, we switched roles.

With a little trepidation, we set off on our adventure. Soon I discovered that I much preferred being the one led. The role of leader made me anxious, as I needed to be responsible not only for myself but someone else's safety.

During my partner's second turn at being led, he became more confident of his ability to walk this trail without my guidance. He began to let go of my elbow for brief moments and graduated to releasing my arm for longer and longer stretches. Using only the sound of my footsteps on the trail as a guide, he began to rely on his sense of hearing to tell him where the path was in space. At one point, he let go for about 30 feet. It was amazing to watch him go from his initial uncertain steps to a new level of surety. I continued to be nervous, however, because I felt responsible for John. It occurred to me that my inability to quell my anxiety was my stuff, specifically my issues around perfection, competency, and control. One time during our switchover in roles, John softly commented that he barely realized that he wasn't touching me. As we traded turns, we expressed great excitement to each other that we were able to trust our blindfolded bodies to walk along the rocky, narrow trail without overt guidance.

At one point, Mark S. came by and suggested that we each selected a stick from the ground to assist in moving bush branches out of the way and mentioned that we would be using them later in the day as our "trouble sticks."

Around midday, we arrived at a massive circle of stones called the "medicine wheel." I was surprised at how large it was. The medicine wheel was nearly 40 feet in diameter, rimmed with rocks that were about two feet high and two feet thick. Inside the circle were more stones, these about a foot high and wide, that dissected the ring into four equal quadrants. It was an imposing and powerful sight. The rocks were aligned so that the four inner lines pointed north, south, east, and west. The Native Americans associated each of these directions with specific parts of the human psyche. Mark told us that north was mind, the south was emotion, east was physical, and west was spiritual. To make access to the circle easier, the builders of this fantastic circle had created an opening in the bordering circumference in the southeast quadrant.

As we walked up towards the wheel, all of us were quietly sharing our blindfold-walk experience with our partners. Once we were all assembled, Mark asked us to sit in a circle facing in and to place our trouble sticks before us. So far, we'd used our trouble sticks only to push branches out of the way of our blindfolded partners. I gazed at my twig and thought about my troubles and the sadness in my life. Once we had quieted down, Mark walked into the middle of the circle and began to lead us into a guided meditation.

"Breathe in deeply," he said between his elongated breaths. "Gently close your eyes and picture the times you've been sad in your life, and as the pictures come in and out of your consciousness, start to note the feelings they bring forth and how the sensations in your body link these pictures and feelings together." After about five minutes of work on this assignment, Mark spoke again. "Note the place within your body where you feel the sensation related to memory. As this place becomes more pronounced within you, focus on this spot where you're feeling the image and see it as something separate from yourself, something that is keeping you from being all that you are. Push the feeling and your description of it out of yourself and into your trouble stick."

As Mark spoke, I conjured up two images that awakened a great sadness in me. First, I'd always felt a desolate emptiness when I'd wondered about my purpose in life. Second, I saw myself chained to my disapproval of myself and the world, to my compulsion to judge just about everything as being wrong, not good enough. I pushed both these feelings into the stick lying on the ground in front of me and felt a wave of relief. Maybe this symbolic gesture had moved me a step closer to finding peace with these torments.

Next, we grabbed our sticks and formed a tight circle within the medicine circle. Then, one by one we walked away and tossed our trouble sticks into a hand-drawn ring in the dirt. We gathered around the small pile of sticks and Mark lit sage smudge and waved it over the sticks as he called for the release of our trouble with a prayer.

After this ritual, we stood in our circle and reflected on our released troubles. I felt greatly liberated. I wasn't yet aware that our journey to freedom was beginning. We looked in the direction of the entrance of the medicine wheel where Mark S. and two other SAGE members, Simon W., and Jeri F., had positioned themselves. Mark faced us and explained the next ceremony. "I'll call you over individually," he said, "and the cords that tie you to others on this planet will be cut by Simon, who will do this by swiftly passing an eagle feather over you. Then Jeri will purify you with a sage smudge, and I'll bind your wrists with leather and blindfold you. At that time, you will enter the medicine wheel to find the place that binds you." Mark then added: "Move slowly around the wheel as you will be blindfolded and will have to traverse the inner rock barriers that divide the circle."

I heard my name called. I wasn't sure what was happening but, eager to take the next step towards enlightenment, I was happy to be the first person to enter the medicine wheel. Simon moved the eagle feather swiftly over my head then down my sides, my front, and my back. Then Jeri swept smoke from the sage smudge all over my body. At last, I walked to Mark at the entrance to the medicine wheel. There he blindfolded me and bound my wrists with a leather string.

It was now up to me to accept the challenge put forth. I was sightless, but my confidence from the blindfold walk had given me courage. With even steps, I crossed the threshold of the medicine wheel and, as instructed, searched for the spot within the area that I sensed was binding me. Mark had told us to listen to the energetic messages we detected coming from the wheel as we moved around it. We would recognize it as "what it is that binds me."

I first walked all the way around the interior edge to get my bearings and to see if I got any particularly strong energetic hits, either positive or negative. I passed by the Western border and quickly realized this wasn't an area that was binding me.

Then I moved North and South and began to look out for a specific feeling of being repelled or being pulled. And there it was. The more I walked toward the north edge, the more it felt as if this was my spot. I slowed down as I homed in on the location where I felt the most pull, then stopped and dug my feet into the ground.

I removed the blindfold and saw that I was in the northernmost (North = Mental) part of the wheel and slightly eastward. This spot felt right. I looked at the ground and sent my mental binding energy and my ego energy straight into the earth. As I did this, I noticed that I was letting myself be distracted by looking around to see if there was maybe a better place in the circle to be. A smile of recognition crept across my face. Ha! I thought. That urge was my mental energy of old not wanting to be released. It was like picking up, setting down, and selecting sticks of wood in Big Sur. I was experiencing the way I let my mind control my actions. Would I be willing to free this compulsion to go and other parts of me, for instance, my emotional and spiritual sides, to have an equal say in the actions I take in my life?

I let this question go for the moment and just let go of my thoughts and grounded myself in the current experience. Quietly, I slipped out of the leather lace binding my wrists, turned towards the entrance to the medicine wheel, picked up my blindfold, and left the circle.

I walked over to the pile of trouble sticks and picked up my trouble stick. I wanted it as a reminder that what binds me is my mind. The lesson was not that I should forgo all mental and rational thoughts and ideas; it was more about running these thoughts past the other aspects of who I am.

With a moment of clarity and lightheartedness, I thought about what my lifelong friend Rick A. use to say to me, about me: "Beware of the man with the lean and hungry look. He thinks too much." It was Rick's slight alteration of a Shakespeare quote from Julius Caesar that he felt suited me to a T.

Now mentally tired, yet feeling that a weight was lifted, I came to this conclusion: "I am both of life and love." I picked up my trouble stick and drew a star in the dirt. In my mind, the symbol represented the light that had shined on me today showing me a way out of sadness.

Mark walked up to me, and we gazed at each other, a slow open smile widening across both our faces. A warm burst of wind came up from the trail leading back down the valley. I turned, and we nodded to each other. It was time for me to go.

I headed back down the trail in this red rock and green tree kingdom, thinking about the clarity growing inside me about myself and how I fit in the universe. I felt ensconced in the spirit of the land, in myself, and in our group.

I'd just witnessed how my mind tends to dominate during decision-making moments, and I contemplated whether this tendency of mine had given me what I wanted in my life. Then I thought about how my emotions rule me when it comes to relationships with women. I would soon learn how this seeming contradiction figured into the whole of my quest for understanding.

What then did the experience in the medicine wheel tell me? That my mind, my logical, analytical mind, made a lot of my decisions, that I rarely checked in with my heart, that I always search for something better, and that I ignored the part of me that ached for peace, joy, and happiness. So where did my emotional relationship with women fit in? I answered this question in the light of today's insights. I had shut out my emotions since childhood, and I didn't understand them.

As a young child, I remember consciously turning off my feelings towards myself and others. I experienced the world outside of my own little body as harsh, cold and uncaring. I realize that my withdrawal from emotions was probably an overreaction to what I had experienced. I can hear my parents' voices telling me that I was "too sensitive" and that I must have been born with this temperament. It was sad to continually get the message from the world that I was just too sensitive. Years of hearing this criticism had taken its toll.

I grew up squelching my feelings and emotions. I became insensitive to others' pain, and I closed myself to the world and the people around me. Not that I didn't have moments of sensitivity and openness, but I was always on my guard for anyone who might attack me.

With these thoughts swirling in my mind, I continued to make my way down the Sedona trail. "What can be done, right now, to help me let go of my reliance on my mind and trust others?" I asked myself. What could I do to gain more trust in my intuition rather than my mind?

Back in the vans, we headed back to the hotel and dinner. Then came our evening session, which Mark had set aside to discuss our individual experiences. My sharing went like this:

"During the walk, up the path with my partner leading me with my blindfold, I had a memory of when I was a little boy and use to walk around the house with my eyes closed. I was always amazed at how well I could do this. Today, having my partner lead me in this way re-opened that memory. It hit me that after childhood my mind took over, keeping me from following an open heart/mind path. Today, for the first time in years, I trusted a more intuitive part of me to guide my steps. It was both fun and reminded me of the wonder I experienced as a child."

After the sharing, we discussed how we acquire expectations and how our minds grow to expect us to behave in certain ways to achieve specific results. We also examined the habits and behaviors to which we tie ourselves to create comfort. But as a dear friend used to say to me: "If you keep doing what you're doing, you'll keep getting what you're getting." Going forward, I wanted to get something different, therefore keeping my eyes open, embracing change and moving out of my comfort zone would be significant.

The SAGE seminars had many workshops on intent and the power of intention to affect what one will experience in life. I want to share one last exercise on purpose from this Master Quest seminar. Although it might seem relatively frivolous, it had a profound impact on me. The training was about the power of belief and the nature of intent and how vital it is to have a clear intention before making decisions.

Mark asked us to identify times we've shrunk from attempting something because we didn't think we could do it. I reflected on jobs I'd not applied for because I didn't believe I had appropriate qualifications. Did I not go for these jobs because I believed I couldn't do them? I had wanted a career in music, but I never got over my fear of singing and playing guitar in public. Did I let my stage fright keep me from putting myself out there in front of people? I was in a high school band, but I blew my chance to follow my dream by getting high during every gig to deaden my fright.

Sharing our fears and doubts out loud with each other in the seminar was powerful. It was fascinating to hear these stories about other people's fears. Sometimes, the concern that my fellow group members revealed seemed silly to me. Then I realized that my apprehensions might look that way to them.

Mark gave each of us two sheets of rice paper and one wooden chopstick. The rice paper was translucent and quite delicate. But when we held it, we discovered that the paper was very strong, not to mention absorbent.

The first and easier challenge was to pierce the rice paper with a chopstick. Working with our partner, in my case with John, one of us to hold one of the two round rice sheets in front of us and horizontal to the ground. The other partner took the chopstick and tried to poke a hole in the rice paper by pressing its small end onto down through the top side of the stretched paper with two fingers. No one succeeded in poking a hole in the paper! But when we moistened the other side of the paper with a few drops of water, everyone got the chopstick easily through the wet part of the paper. This phase of the challenge seemed almost silly. Then we embarked on the second phase.

Mark asked; "could the rice paper break the wooden chopstick?" Most all of us laughed and said, "no way. Paper can't break a stick!"

Mark reminded us of the earlier Magic Maker workshop when we broke wooden boards with our hands, first with brute force, then softly with clear intention. During that workshop, Peggy and Bill had spoken at length about using the power of intention to overcome our internal mental obstacles. Their talks were peppered with stories about people overcoming beliefs that something couldn't be done.

So, we had to take this challenge seriously. I looked at my partner and smiled. We would use our intention to make this happen. Mark told us to fold the rice paper in half to create an even folded edge. The folded edge would be used to strike the chopstick. I asked John if I could make the first attempt with the rice paper. My visualization had given me a powerful feeling about my being able to do this.

John and I focused on the rice paper in my hands and the chopstick in his hand, and I pictured the rice paper breaking through the stick.

John picked up the chopstick and held it as instructed between his two thumbs and forefingers, his other fingers curled into a fist. It was a steady and robust position, fortunate because having a stable anchored target was essential.

Placing my folded rice paper edge on the chopstick, I visualized the rice paper passing through the chopstick. After about 45 seconds of running this vision over and over again in my mind, I raised the rice paper to about 18 inches above the stick and with one clear fast motion brought the edge of the rice paper down onto the chopstick.

With a definite "crack" the wooden chopstick broke. Both my heart and mind almost leaped out of my body. I was both amazed and thrilled. I wouldn't have believed this if someone had told me they'd broken a stick with piece of paper. Feeling very empowered, I felt seeds of what I might do in this life drop into the soil of my soul.

The Magic Quest course provided many different themes that opened doors for exploration and growth. I was amazed by the joy I derived from the Sedona, AZ session, and I knew that I would be back on my own to do further exploration.

I drove away from Sedona with my mind energetically compiling a to-do list for my new life:

1. Give up my apartment and live homeless for a while to see where it takes me.
2. Detail a specific plan for a book.
3. Visit my parents, brother, and his family with the objective of better understanding them and giving them the opportunity to understand me.
4. Perform miracles with friends and family whenever possible.
5. Resolve my SAGE contract issues with Bill.

Thoughts also flooded through my head about the wisdom I had acquired from my SAGE experience:

- Consciousness creates.
- I've created who I am.
- I've created my reality.
- I'm always standing at the edge of my future.
- I can make better choices in my life by:
    o Being aware of what it feels like to be where you want to be.
    o Being aware of what is like to arrive at where you want to be.
- Emotion is energy in motion (e-motion).
- Ego is constantly fighting for its life and justification.
- In my quest to know someone else, I often run into me.
- It makes sense to listen to you.

- The Victim Game consists of victim, persecutor, and rescuer. If I am playing one of these roles, I am participating in the game.
- A Rilke quote: "I feel it now... there's a power in me to grasp and give shape to my world. I know that nothing has ever been real without my beholding it."

In a reflection of the SAGE courses I had taken, I found them slightly crazy yet inspiring because they pushed me, and others, past the edges of our comfort zone to see where there was courage, potential, and wisdom lying below our fears.

Chapter 12

Miracles? Maybe...

Nearly 15 months had gone by since I read that *Wall Street Journal* ad for SAGE and it was now early summer of 1990. Bill and Peggy had welcomed me into the SAGE training program and promised me that soon I'd be producing and leading workshops. Meanwhile, my life situation had become challenging. I had sold or given away my remaining possessions and made my lifestyle spare and straightforward.

I was sleeping in my car or on floors, beds, or couches in the homes of friends. Often, I used a local gym as a place to shower and clean up. I had a telephone number connected to a voicemail-only system, and my mail delivered to a "Mail Boxes Etc." in San Francisco. The last SAGE training had drained a good portion of my remaining bank account, a factor that added to my very free-flowing, unencumbered lifestyle.

This situation made me especially eager to start work as a SAGE seminar leader. Because the San Francisco Bay Area territories were sold, and my financial situation was limited, I partnered with two others, Michael B. and Helene F., to purchase SAGE's Pacific Northwest region. Michael was originally from the Portland area, and I had a close affinity for the whole Pacific Northwest. The understanding was that the three of us would each own a third and build a SAGE regional business in this area.

I had met Michael, a slight, intellectual-looking resident of the Bay Area who was married to a police officer, early in my experience with SAGE. Besides doing dyads together, we'd spent time discussing the business model, and had met with Bill and his team at the SAGE offices in Rohnert Park. Helene was a slender, stylish woman in her mid-forties, married to a Berkeley ophthalmologist; she drove a British racing green Jaguar and had two kids, one of them adopted. One thing that connected us was that we both had adopted children. She had also attended a number of the same SAGE seminars that I'd participated in.

As a team, our first goal to develop the region was to put on one-day introductory seminars. We bought ads in newspapers, lined up a hotel meeting room, and proceeded to respond to telephone calls from our ads. Doing this from afar was somewhat challenging, but our efforts paid off in the form of a very successful introductory seminar at a Red Lion Hotel in Seattle with about 22 people in attendance. We gave a short opening talk and did a couple of brief forgiveness exercises and had lots of one-on-one engagement with our participants. At the end of our presentation, nine of the participants signed up for a SAGE Corporate Dreamwalk seminar scheduled for the upcoming month. For this work, we received a small commission check. We were on our way and felt good on our long drive back to the bay area together.

However, this ended up being the full extent of our SAGE business-building efforts because Michael and I were running out of money. If we couldn't put on a lot more introductory seminars and hold a few well-attended Dreamwalk seminars, we'd run entirely out of money before the business was profitable. Helene was prosperous, and she offered to help Michael and me. However, we did not feel comfortable tapping into her resources to support this effort. Besides, another last-nail-in-the-coffin event led us to decide to halt our SAGE endeavors.

SAGE had sold Michael, Helene, and me the Pacific Northwest region. Then, without telling us, it sold the same area to another person who was from Vancouver, B.C. My guess was, this man had a lot of money, and Bill saw him as someone who would be able to add more dollars to the corporate SAGE kitty.

When we heard about the Vancouver investor in "our" territory, I hopped into my car, drove up to Rohnert Park, and stormed into the SAGE offices. Forgetting most of my resolutions to be kind, I barged into Bill's office and lit into him about this breach of trust and his greedy ways. I continued my harangue with all the things I saw wrong with his organization and how he managed it, and I ended with my feelings that SAGE, specifically Bill, lacked honesty, especially since his actions did not align with what he preached. Bill was stunned. With tears welling up in his eyes, he started giving me a sad story to justify his fraudulent behavior, but at this point, I couldn't trust him any longer. I left the SAGE offices knowing I'd never be back and that my career as a Sage Master was over.

I was very disappointed, hurt, and angry at the lack of integrity in an outfit that I had trusted with my innermost self. It was especially hurtful that SAGE promoted open truthfulness as part of the path and yet Bill wasn't truthful or transparent himself. It reminded me of the adage that you teach what you most need to learn.

At the same time, I recognized that I'd acquired knowledge and skills as a transformational leader, and I couldn't help being grateful to SAGE for guiding me forward on my transformation. Although my dream of delivering personal growth seminars through SAGE dashed, my prospects for continuing along this path were not only still there and possibly, even more, promising now that I was a free agent.

Helene and her husband had the financial wherewithal to threaten SAGE with a lawsuit for this territory contract violation. To avoid spending a lot of money to defend a suit, Bill gave us back our $10,000. I appreciated Helene's assistance in getting back our money. Considering the state of my finances, this would be helpful. I had sold most everything I owned and didn't have much in the way of prospects for work because I'd been out of the official job market for nearly two years.

Later, I learned that SAGE had to settle Federal Trade Commission (FTC) charges of falsely representing the growth and money-making possibilities of their business and business model. They were "banned from the sale or marketing of any franchise or similar business venture and from offering employment opportunities for which they charge money."

Regardless of SAGE's failings, it had enabled me to shift two significant impediments to contentment in my life, my relationship with my parents and my level of spiritual awareness. SAGE had moved the needle significantly on these two fronts. The latter shift was jolted loose in many of the SAGE workshops and steadied by my evolving daily Vipassana meditation practice. Lastly, I was committed to sitting at more meditation retreats, attending personal growth seminars, and exploring the myriad materials published about spirituality and personal growth.

When it came to finding a new base for my spiritual quest—and possibly an opportunity to use my new skills—I was lucky to be living in Marin County, California in the late 80s and early 90s. Here, I didn't have to look far. I soon started participating in a meditation group held in a church in Fairfax on Monday nights. The lead teacher was Jack Kornfield, a notable figure in the American Buddhist meditation world. A slender man with a receding hairline and tremendously kind, intense eyes, Jack was indeed a charismatic speaker. And here he was, right around the corner from where I parked my car. Although I could not meet regularly with this group because I was planning to leave the area to spend time with my parents, I knew I would reconnect at some future point.

Visiting my parents was something that came up during several SAGE workshops. I felt as though I had unfinished business with them, and one way to begin to resolve this would be to spend time with them, be curious, and learn more about them. In return, it might be possible that they'd want to know more about me.

The inner quiet that was growing inside me because of recent experiences and my meditation practice was starting to change my outward behavior. For one, my displays of anger were shifting toward patience and understanding. Self-inquiry had rewarded me with a changed demeanor. I now understood that my short temper and anger originated in my sadness, sorrow, and hurt. Incorporating this new awareness into my meditation practice, I suffered fewer angry moments and was better able to see through to the hurt within me.

The other avenue I pursued to enhance my spiritual awakening was reading. With the plethora of spiritual and personal growth books available, it was difficult to select just a few, so I immersed myself in an eclectic range of books.

Numerous people had recommended one of the publications that interested me most over the last six months. It was called *A Course in Miracles* (ACIM), published by the Foundation for Inner Peace. The teachings in this book are Christian-based. One of its authors, Helen Schucman, said that she "received" the ACIM material from a voice. She thereby does not take credit for the book's contents. Quoted as saying, "Although Christian in statement, the Course deals with universal spiritual themes." Helen wrote down the information she received from the voice in shorthand, and her partner, William Thetford, then transcribed the material into *A Course in Miracles*.

I was drawn to this material because I had heard from others who had taken "The Course" that it was astonishing and compelling. Despite its Christian foundation, I had gathered from others that the teachings were not dogmatically Christian.

I vividly remember the sunny late summer day in August of 1990 that I walked into Open Secret, a bookstore on C Street in San Rafael, California. In this bookstore was a multitude of spiritually oriented books, crystal, and brass singing bowls, and other assorted "new age" stuff. As I walked among the shelves of inviting books, I was looking for just one, the *A Course in Miracles*, and there it was, in a dark blue cover with gold lettering, with the look and feel of a soft-cover Bible. I eyed the book but felt reluctant to pick it up. Feelings of doubt swirled inside me. Was I about to give myself up to a set of values to which I didn't identify? I certainly didn't want to be linked with the Christian path as it currently manifested itself in the world. I strongly disagreed with many tenets of the Christian religion, among them that you were supposed to be "God-fearing."

My understanding of "God" (or whatever term one may use) was closer to the concept of life being a singularity of light. How could God, an entity I think of as perfection, light, life, and benevolence, have anything to do with fear (False Experience Appearing Real)? To me, fear is man's creation, not something created by a God. Other aspects of Christian-based teachings also repelled me. Christians say that it is righteous to kill in the name of God, that God sends people to Hell, that there are sins and sinners, and that God punishes the sinners. Deep within myself, I knew that no real God, as I conceived of it, would bestow upon humanity such a cruel and arbitrary system of values.

Something else was going on deep inside me that day because, despite my misgivings, I decided to buy this book even though it looked like a Bible.

Picking it up from the shelf, I opened to the preface. I was encouraged to read that Helen had been an atheist when she started to receive the material. Just as reassuring was her description of herself as a "psychologist, educator, conservative in theory and atheistic in belief...." Schucman probably had stronger negative feelings than did I toward formal religions, including Christianity. Considering her freedom from religious dogma of any kind, her claim to have "received" a very thick body of information led me to believe that there might be something here for me to learn. It was compelling that Helen hadn't expected to receive this information but took it upon herself, over a seven-year period, to record and share the material with others.

Reading on, I learned that The Course consisted of three parts: The Text, Workbook for Students (the lessons), and Manual for Teachers. The Text covers the theory and the concepts used in the Course. The Workbook for Students lists 365 lessons, one for each day of the year. And the Manual for Teachers provides a list of answers to questions students may have as they go through ACIM.

I was especially intrigued to read that ACIM helps readers distinguish what is real from what isn't real. I strongly felt that people tend to distort the truth by erecting defenses against it. Take, for example, the concept of original sin. As preached to me in churches, original sin was part of being human. To me, this meant that the moment we were born we were living in a negative state. I didn't believe there is such a thing as sin, nor could I imagine that God would inflict such an adverse condition on his creation, humankind.

Then there were the Ten Commandments. Christian churches teach that we are sinners if we violate any one of them. This moral code struck me as unfair since every person is a work in progress and not perfect—an acceptable condition entirely separate from the guilt and fear of sin.

In ACIM sin is defined differently from what's commonly taught. Sin doesn't exist in ACIM's reality. It is instead the absence of something. According to ACIM, "Sin is defined as 'lack of love.' Since love is all there is, sin in the sight of the Holy Spirit is a mistake to be corrected, rather than an evil to be punished." This view of sin and love resonated strongly with me because until then, I'd heard about sin only from priests, fathers, ministers and lay people who projected themselves as religiously righteous. Reading this fantastic new understanding of sin made the old teachings about it seem twisted and dense. I would agree that sin of old was put forth to control people, a way to always dangle the threat of punishment before humanity. I stood in the aisle of the bookshop, mesmerized. Every page I read struck me as if someone was accurately throwing darts into my soul.

The preface finishes with two paragraphs on forgiveness that brought tears to my eyes. Three sentences, in particular, spoke to me: "Through forgiveness the thinking of the world is reversed. The forgiven world becomes the gate of Heaven because by its mercy we can, at last, forgive ourselves. Holding no one prisoner to guilt, we become free." These powerful words corroborated the recent teachings on forgiveness at the SAGE seminars.

As I read, I slowly sank against the edge of the bookshelf, ending up on the floor paging through more of the book. I flipped through some of the Text, Workbook, and Manual sections and started thinking that if I bought this book, I would have to finish it. I could not do this halfway. I needed to be willing to receive what it could teach me, and for that to happen, I would have to be open to the experience, no matter my reticence about Christian-based thought.

I turned back to the Introduction to the Text and reread it. This time, the first five sentences made me smile: "This is a course in miracles," it said. "It is a required course. Only the time you take it is voluntary. Free will does not mean that you can establish the curriculum. It means that you can select what you want to take at a given time."

This statement was right in line with the very first lesson in the ACIM Workbook section, which states: "Nothing I see in this room (on this street, from this window, in this place) means anything." I understood this to mean that the value and importance we put on those things are not real.

What is real is something more encompassing than the things sitting outside of ourselves. What is real is the truth of things as they are. As the introduction states, "The purpose of the workbook is to train your mind in a systematic way to a different perception of everyone and everything in the world. If true perception has been achieved in connection with any person, situation or event, total transfer to everyone and everything is certain. On the other hand, one exception held apart from true perception makes its accomplishments anywhere impossible." This declaration reinforced my perception that ACIM was something all-encompassing and that it was a gateway to learning to see things as they are. It was also in line with my understanding of what my budding daily meditation practice was all about: Already it was focusing on seeing what is real, beyond the pre-defined objects in the outside world.

I read a little of the introduction to the last section, "Manual For Teachers." As with the other sections of the book, a couple of sentences immediately resonated with me. "The course…emphasizes that to teach *is* to learn, so that teacher and learner are the same. It also emphasizes that teaching is a constant process; it goes on every moment of the day, and continues into sleeping thoughts as well."

By now more than an hour had gone by while I nosed around numerous sections and pages of this book. With a deep breath, I decided to buy it. I was already thinking about how I would absorb all three segments and complete the 365 daily lessons throughout the next year.

The day after I bought the book, I set a date to begin the journey. The reader was instructed to complete one lesson a day for a year. The Workbook for Students forbids explicitly undertaking more than one lesson a day. Therefore, I decided to read the Text and Manual for Teachers at the same time, with the goal of finishing all three sections of the Course at about the same time.

On my self-appointed first day, I started with Lesson One, entitled: "Nothing I see…means anything." The instructions said it should not take me more than a minute to execute the lesson and to do it again. So there I was, sitting in my car on an early autumn morning carrying out the lesson. As instructed, I looked around at where I was, the interior of my car, then outside, beyond the windows, and said: "That speedometer does not mean anything. That handle does not mean anything. That knob does not mean anything. That sign does not mean anything. That bridge does not mean anything." I did this for a little over a minute, feeling both amusement and a reverent seriousness. The amusement came from looking at things I could touch and see and saying out loud, "this gear shift/steering wheel/tree aren't real and don't mean anything." This simple exercise was giving me a direct means to begin deconstructing the outside world and my attachments to it.

Along with my commitment to completing the lessons in one year, I had also committed myself to finish the Text and Manual in the same year regardless of any other eventualities that might arise. The Text was by far the most substantial part of the book, so after completing the first lesson, I dived right into it.

The text begins with a list of 50 Principles of Miracles. As I read through the list, some of these principles jumped out at me, among them this one: "There is no order of difficulty in miracles. One is not 'harder' or 'bigger' than another. They are all the same. All expressions of love are maximal." I read this to mean that love is the currency for all miracles and that any being who uses this currency can manifest a miracle. A miracle can be made by smiling at someone who is having a challenging moment, so he or she transcends into a relaxed joy. A miracle could be caused by two opposing governments that come together to assist in the rescue of people lost or hurt by an earthquake. In the realm of miracles, neither is better, harder, or more significant than the other.

Many of the principles reminded me of stories that I'd heard from history and stories from my own life. One ACIM principle stated, "The use of miracles as spectacles to induce belief is a misunderstanding of their purpose." The historical story that came to mind about this principle was from the Bible, John 6:2-6:14, which states that thousands of people were fed with only five barley loaves and two small fishes. The point of this event was not to invent a story to convert people; it was to feed hungry people.

Another of the principles that brought up a personal story was, "A miracle is a service. It is the maximal service you can render to another. It is a way of loving your neighbor as yourself. You recognize your own and your neighbor's work simultaneously."

Between 1984 through 1991, I was motivated to do community service. While serving food at St. Anthony's Dining Room, I met Robert (Bob) T., a former Folsom prisoner who was now doing prison outreach. He invited me to get involved with a program in which I began to communicate with prisoners either in person or by mail. I engaged with several prisoners over those years and spent numerous hours in the visiting rooms of San Quentin and Folsom prisons, meeting with prisoners as a friend and someone in which they could confide. I also wrote to prisoners who wanted to communicate with someone outside the walls. To this day I continue to correspond by email with one former prisoner, though he is currently living in his home country of Iran. The joy I receive when I hear from him is incredible: In those moments he is I and I am he. We are one.

The last one of the ACIM principles I'll cite here is this one about freedom: "A major contribution of miracles is their strength in releasing you from your false sense of isolation, deprivation, and lack." Therefore, when miracles move us into the realm of revelation, we are no longer in isolation. In the field of revelation, we are filled with love and therefore cannot be deprived of anything because everything that is real is there for us in the realm of love. Lastly, in this realm where everything exists, there cannot be any feeling of deprivation.

In the above paragraphs, I've spoken about revelation as a state of being. Revelation in straight biblical terms refers to the last book of the New Testament. There have been many dissertations, papers, and theoretical analysis of the book of Revelations. I do not intend here to interpret the bible, but only to clarify ACIM's use of the word "revelation." In ACIM's vernacular, revelation is experienced only in consciousness. As the Course states: "Revelation unites you directly with God." It is a timeless state in which peace, freedom, and love exist. When one sees and embodies the truth of what is, one experiences revelation, a realization of oneness with all.

During this personal journey to personal freedom, I was looking for a revelation, the revelation of my life. And although the Course describes revelation uniting one with God, I didn't think of it as being with "God" as it is generally believed of today. What this picture of revelation looked like to me was an internal peace, freedom from encumbrances, and actions based on love. I wanted to reveal myself to myself.

Chapter 13

Forgiveness - My First Principle of Freedom

The Workbook lessons of *A Course in Miracles* are divided into two major sections. As I worked through the lessons, it became clear why the lessons are split this way. The first section is designed to undo the way the student sees the world. The second is designed to teach a "true perception" of the world. To this end, most lessons first address specific subjects or perceptions and then systematically point toward another way to view the world. Spaced between groupings in the first section are review lessons that reinforce the aims of each group. In the second section, lessons are grouped by specific subjects such as "What is forgiveness?" "What is Sin?" "What is the Body?" "What is the Real World?" "What is the Ego?" "What is a Miracle?" and "What am I?"

In the Text section of ACIM, there is a sentence that states: "You who want peace can find it only by complete forgiveness." I mentioned earlier that I believe forgiveness is one way to find freedom because it starts to free up the mind from unresolved grievances or issues in our life. Because only love is real, and everything else is an illusion, forgiveness is the acknowledgment that what you thought you did to yourself or what you did to your brother or sister didn't happen. Conversely, it recognizes that whatever your brother or sister did to you did not happen either. In the Course, there is a sentence that sums up the results of forgiveness. It states: "The holiest of all the spots on earth is where an ancient hatred has become a present love." Forgiving another allows any grievance, even an old hatred, to transport one into peace, love, and freedom.

To be clear, I don't believe that forgiveness means condoning harsh and insensitive behavior. The forgiveness that ACIM teaches has the power to heal. At a SAGE training, Mark had shared a similar concept of forgiveness with us in the form of a Hawaiian word that describes a forgiving spirit so powerful that it heals both the forgiven and the forgiver. The word is "Ho'oponopono," which means to make right or to rectify an error. It is like our phrase "make amends." In the traditional Hawaiian culture, errors arise from thoughts that are tainted by painful, unforgiven memories from the past which then cause imbalance and disease. Ho'oponopono offers a way to release the energy of these painful thoughts or errors. I grasped that the Hawaiian word and the ACIM Workbook expressed the same concept, that personal transformation begins with forgiveness. Forgiveness then became the first step on my journey into freedom. Embracing forgiveness became my first principle of freedom:

Forgiveness
Freedom requires that I can forgive myself and others.

Forgiveness results in acceptance of the past as it happened. If I cannot forgive fully and freely, then freedom will not be readily available. An unforgiven event keeps me tied to the event and drives all current and future decision-making and behavior. I'm not saying that one cannot experience brief glimmers of freedom without having wholly forgiven all unforgiven events in my life. Without true forgiveness, however, those moments will be transitory. Life exists for giving.

You can find an excellent analogy to the effects of having unforgiven events in one's life in the introduction to Dr. Fred Luskin's book *Forgive for Good*. Luskin asks us to visualize both day-to-day issues and unresolved grievances of our life as airplanes blinking on an air traffic controllers' screen. Keeping track of all these planes on the radar screen requires us to use a lot of mental power. Landing the airplanes of day-to-day issues helps free up mental space. If the aircraft that represent unresolved grievances or unforgiven events keep flying, they continue to hijack our mind space. As time goes by, more and more of these unresolved grievances stack up on our air traffic control screen, appropriating more and more of our mental capacity. Luskin says, "Having them [your unresolved grievances] on the screen forces you to work harder and increases the chance of accidents."

A grievance is what happens when you are living with an unresolved issue in your life. And if this grievance isn't resolved—if the plane hasn't landed—then one needs to call on additional internal resources to keep track of it. Dr. Luskin goes on to say, "Forgiveness is the peace you learn to feel when you allow these circling planes to land." Freedom means all your planes have landed and your radar screen is flawless.

ACIM declares, "The real world is attained simply by the complete forgiveness of the old, the world you see without forgiveness." It goes on to say, "All this beauty will rise to bless your sight as you look upon the world with forgiving eyes. Forgiveness transforms vision and lets you see the real world reaching quietly and gently across chaos, removing all illusions that had twisted your perception and fixed it on the past."

Reading ACIM, I began to look at life differently. By releasing unforgiven past moments and events, I could come to see the world as it is and not as I had seen it through the filters of actions—my own and others'—that I'd not forgiven.

I realized at the start of my journey that everything we experience leaves an imprint in our brain. Therefore, if I had unresolved grievances (planes in the air), they would overload my circuits, reducing my freedom to make choices. I would be using valuable internal resources to stay aloft instead of using them to embrace my life curriculum. As the Course states: "Forgiveness takes away what stands between your brother and yourself."

The power of forgiveness has been demonstrated scientifically. Research has found that people who have a forgiving nature have fewer health problems and have less stress than average. And as Alexander Pope wrote: "Good-nature and good sense must ever join; to err is human, to forgive divine."

Looking in the mirror one day as I was brushing my teeth at the gym, I silently asked myself, "What and whom do I need to forgive?" What planes did I still have in the air? I immediately started thinking of actions and people outside of me that I wanted to forgive.

I made a list of people I needed to forgive. There had been times when I might have consciously and unconsciously hurt these people with my words and/or actions. Walking out into the gym's parking lot, I realized there were still plenty of things for which I needed to forgive myself as well. I sat in my car, suddenly paralyzed by floods of thoughts that hit me about things I'd done that I regretted. "This is the place to start," a voice said, from where or from whom I don't know. But I knew what the voice meant. "Start with yourself." I had to forgive myself before I could forgive others.

These past few months, I'd already made a lot of progress on this front. I had forgiven my parents, a big step, for contributing to my feelings of being unloved as a child. Now I had to face forgiving myself, and there was a lot to forgive.

One of the biggest planes on my air traffic controller screen was the hurt and sadness I carried with me from killing other human beings. I had previously worked with my grief over this reality, but I had not yet succeeded in fully forgiving myself for killing a man, especially the first. That soldier was someone's son, possibly a father, maybe an uncle, and even worse, like me, he could have been a dad.

When I think about the thousands of people who met their deaths from the artillery I fired or from my rifle fire or the bombings of large areas I approved, including villages, I felt sick to my stomach. Not only did I slay "the enemy," I killed part of myself by my acts. I'm sure there were woman and children died as well.

When I would tell these stories and feelings to other people, most of them would say to me that killing those people wasn't my fault because I was under the control and direction of the U.S. Army and as a soldier, it was my responsibility to follow orders.

Their comments were valid at one level, and yes, the Army trained me to kill people. But that doesn't mean that doing it was okay or the right thing to do. The fact that my government ordered me to slay people they deemed the enemy does not condone the killing, and it was especially painful for me because I believed that the entire war I fought was a terrible mistake. Worse, when it came time to pull the trigger, I had a choice. I could have said "no" to requests for bombing specific targets. I could have said no, taken a court-martial, gone to an Army brig and served my time for my beliefs. However, I didn't have the inner strength to do this, as one of my heroes, Muhammad Ali, did.

The act of forgiving, I realized, varies depending on the seriousness or complexity of the perceived transgression. Sometimes, forgiving requires us to make an honest heart-filled statement: "I forgive you for …" or "Michael, I forgive you for…." At other times, the process of forgiveness is more complicated, and we may need to ask a therapist, teacher, elder, or spiritual leader to help us identify the right kernel that requires a release. Of course, for any act of forgiveness to be effective, it needs to be done with conviction. The plane on the radar screen needs to land, not just moved to a lower altitude.

These insights led me to understand that forgiveness at all levels requires three acts of courage. First, we need to be willing to accept responsibility for our part in the action and behavior. Second, we need to have an honest understanding of what we are forgiving. Third, we need to be clear about the look and feel with the outcome of our forgiveness.

Again, forgiving is not about expecting someone else to change their behavior or what they feel. And our goal cannot be to change someone's perception of what someone thinks about us. The purpose of forgiveness is to become free of the unresolved grievance.

Therefore, my goal wasn't to picture the dead man's family opening their heart or arms toward me in a gesture of forgiveness. It was for me to feel unburdened by the thoughts of taking his life. My goal was not to continue to punish myself for the actions I made years ago. It was to know I learned from the events of that time and would not repeat them. My goal was to accept my actions without condoning or forgetting that the events happened. It is to let go of the chains that bound me to those previous actions and to do this with reverence and grace.

I knew of two changes that would result from this particular action: I would not have guns in my life, and I would never again take another person's life. Going forward, I was clear that I would give up my own life rather than take another's. It isn't that I don't value my life, but I also know that life is transitory and that my assignment is to live it with integrity.

My new forgiveness practice came to include writing down the motivations behind my wish to forgive. For each act of forgiveness, I wrote a simple statement about the action I was forgiving and the result I wanted. These notes helped me to keep my intentions clear.

My advice to those embarking on a practice of forgiveness is first to look deeply into your intentions, then to write your simple statement describing the result you want. Pause for a moment, breathe slowly, and envision your purpose. Finally, in a clear voice that comes from both your heart and mind, make your forgiveness statement. In my case, it was, "I forgive myself for killing others while I was in the Army."

Since then I have made this statement many more times. Today, years later, I find that I can sometimes speak of those events without deep sadness. Still, at other times I am less successful in detaching myself emotionally from those memories. The memory always arrives, however, without guilt. Herein lies freedom.

Chapter 14

Work – It's Not What, But How

It was now late 1990, and I'd been living without a home, in and out of my car, for about seven months. I had been following my daily meditation practice strictly for most of that time and was happy to feel it making a difference. Meditation had helped me see more easily through to the root-cause of my actions, to become more compassionate, and to feel at peace with my past.

Meanwhile, the daily *Course in Miracles* lessons that I'd been doing for about eight months was working well with my daily meditation practice. It was time for me to re-engage with the world where I could put into practice what I'd learned about forgiveness. I still had a few planes flying around on my radar screen and wanted to land them.

Some of these planes were carrying unresolved memories that involved my parents. My best chance to get those planes off my radar screen was to spend time with them.

Generally, I was very guarded as a child. I had felt as if no one except my paternal grandmother understood how sensitive I was. To protect myself from continually being hurt, I built a harsh and unfriendly exterior. In fact, in my family, there was a reference to my giving "the look," which expressed disapproval of anyone probing how I might be thinking or feeling. At age 17, I had run away from home, and shortly after that left it for good and joined the Army. Despite being sad, hurt, and unhappy about my childhood, I loved my parents and had always hoped that there would be a time when I could open my heart fully to them. It now was a perfect moment to work on my forgiveness practice and reach out to them.

I started preparing for this trip by relooking at my SAGE genogram, the personality-focused family tree that Simon had had us create during the Magic Maker workshop. The genogram laid out the history of my family from generations back. With it open in front of me, I could see the origins of my parents' rigid child-raising methods. As I began to understand their lives better, my compassion for them grew.

In late October of 1990, I drove the 262 miles from the Larkspur Landing parking lot in Marin County, California, where I'd been sleeping, to Morro Bay on the Central California coast, where my parents lived. My goal was to understand better where I came from and to do this with an open heart in the heart of their home.

Walking into their house that late Sunday afternoon, I sensed a little trepidation about what I was doing there. On my way to dropping my bag in the guest room, I saw that my mom had made the sofa bed into a bed. Dad was watching a football game. Mom talked about what she was going to make for dinner.

At dinner, I told them I wanted to know about their past and what they knew about their family history. I started by relaying many of the words I'd heard them use in casual conversations about their parents and grandparents. Although both my mother and father came from small homes, my mother's side had a history of large families, up to 12 children. I quipped that as practicing French Catholics, they fulfilled the perception that the French were lovers, and, as Catholics, had no love for birth control.

As I quoted them saying "tough as nails," "hard-working," and "nose to the grindstone" I elicited laughs and nodding smiles and created space for them to discuss their families. My dad talked about the harsh winters of South Dakota and how he had to spend a lot of time alone because his dad was gone 90 percent of the time and his mother worked. Being an only child, and captive their snowed-in house, allowed his imagination to grow. He experimented with building things in their work shed. I know he learned a lot because he was extremely good at designing and building things in our home. I marveled at his ability to take a problem, analyze it, and create solutions.

One time he designed and built a camping unit that slid into the back of our 1957 Plymouth station wagon. What was unique about it became apparent once we pulled in to our camping spot. The unit would roll all the way out of the back of the wagon except for six inches resting on the tailgate. Metal legs unfolded to support the outer end. Then we would extend a tarp from that end all the way to the back of the station wagon. Now that the space inside the station wagon was effectively doubled, our whole family could sleep in it.

Additionally, my dad built a large dark green box for the end farthest from the car. The box, with doors on the sides and back, held our stove, food, water storage, and camping utensils, and, with additional legs, it could stand on its own if we decided to leave the campground and take the car for a day of sightseeing.

The final ingenious part of the contraption was that it had eye hooks on the top so that when we got home, we could attach it to a rope and pulley system and raise the whole unit to the rafters in the garage.

It was amazing to watch my father think up, draw, and build things like this.

My mom painted abstract expressionist art in watercolor and acrylic paints, and she liked to walk on the beach. It was one of her favorite things to do. During my visit, walking with her was an excellent way to catch her by herself. On one of our walks, she told me a story that exemplified some of the differences between my parents' paths in life and my mine.

When my mother turned 16 years old, her father told her that she was to quit school and work full time in the local woolen mill in her town of Northbridge, Massachusetts. Her entire family and the whole town worked in these mills. She had been working there already during high school summer vacations. Her father thought that girls didn't need an education and insisted that she should work full time as soon as she turned 16, the legal age for full-time employment in the mills. He never asked her what she wanted. She had wanted to finish high school, maybe even go to college, and to have a life different from the one her parents had.

My mother's story wasn't uncommon for many girls in 1939, especially in that part of the country. Because she lived in a deeply religious Catholic community, she went to Catholic school where the nuns were very strict and unkind to their students, and particularly cruel to children who were left-handed, like my mom. In those days, the belief was that the left hand was the hand of the devil. To rectify this and set the child straight, each time a child attempted to write with her left hand, a nun would come by and rap that side with a ruler. My mom still writes with her right hand but does almost everything else with her left side. This sort of intolerance and cruelty from the nuns was one reason that my mom had no use for religion and very rarely took us to church.

Additionally, my parents grew up during the Great Depression when life was hard on many levels. It stands to reason that the pain they suffered showed up when they were parents raising their children. I knew they only wanted the best for me, for me to have as much as possible because they had so little.

I stayed with them for nearly two months. In that time, I felt I gained a better understanding of them. On their side, they continued to be the two people they were and did not reciprocate my interest in them. That was OK with me. My intent in visiting was to understand them and my feelings toward them better, so I wasn't going to stay any longer and attempt to change them. I didn't want to overstay my welcome. Besides, I had not held a job for nearly two years, and my previously thin bank account was starved.

From when I started working in high school, I'd bought my clothes and paid for almost all my possessions and extracurricular activities. After joining the Army, I'd taken care of all my financial needs and assumed that I could continue to support myself in some way.

However, my latest venture with SAGE had required me to dip into all my reserves, and I was homeless. I needed to work. Before now, I had never worried about finding work. My college degree in Social Ecology with a minor in psychology from the University of California, Irvine, had served me well enough in the corporate world. I also had a wealth of experience. I had worked in various management and consulting positions at Bank of America, including managing the Credit Card Customer Service Division and serving as a senior operational and systems consultant for the bank's consumer division.

Additionally, I had managed large and complex business systems projects for Associates National Bank and served as Director of Management Information Systems at AT&E, the start-up company that I'd been laid off from at the beginning of this journey. I had performed exceptionally well at these companies and was fairly paid, but I had not enjoyed the work. It began to gnaw and nag at me that I had never found a calling that I connected with and that the one time I thought I'd be contributing to others' personal growth, it didn't work out.

Just as I had dreamed on my camping trip of having a job that made me feel that I was contributing something beautiful to the world while making a lot of money, I was touching on that same feeling now.

People who love their work are always telling others to "do what you love." My problem was that I didn't have a clue about what I might like, let alone love. Now, with a newfound understanding of myself, I was hoping a new door would open.

Still, in Morro Bay, I decided one day as I walked along the water's edge to sit in meditation near one of the sand berms on the upper part of the beach. After about 40 minutes of sitting, I got up and headed back toward the ocean before I went to the car. Approaching the shoreline, I looked out at the setting sun and had this epiphany: Many people achieve fulfillment in a job regardless of *what* the position is. They find satisfaction in *how* they do it.

A massive wave of relief flowed through my body. By the time I reached my car, I was almost giddy with joy. I could find any job and incorporate what I was learning about myself into the *how* of doing the work.

It was early December. The New Year was just around the corner. Companies would be working on their budgets, and new positions would be available. I'd start my search in the morning.

I never got to start my job search. The very next morning, I found a message on my answering machine: "Hi, Michael. This is Dennis M. A little over two years ago; you sent us your resume for a consulting position with our project management software company. We are now ready to move our presence out to the West, and we would like to interview you for one of our consulting positions. Please give me a call."

Well, I can't begin to tell you the size of my smile at hearing this message. I listened to it again to make sure I heard it right and then listened to it a third time. Then I wrote down the telephone number. The company that had offered me the interview was ABT Corporation, which stood for Applied Business Technology, Inc., a maker and seller of project management software tools with a new branch office in San Francisco.

Dennis was what some would call a "good ol' boy" from Texas. We set up a time for a formal phone interview. His voice was kind, with a southwest accent, and after we discussed consulting, project management, and systems development, I could tell he knew what he was talking about and he knew that I knew what I was talking about. But, more importantly, there was a level of integrity that came across over the phone that I loved. The process, he said, would be a phone interview followed by a face-to-face meeting. If offered the position, I'd start on January 1. After the phone interview, I felt confident that I would do well in the face-to-face.

If I got an offer, it would be great to have San Francisco as my home and base while traveling to client sites four to five days a week.

What concerned me about taking this job was that I was in the middle of doing the daily lessons in ACIM, and I wasn't willing to stop doing them. I also wanted to continue my meditation practice, which was giving me peace, joy, and a taste of freedom. I wondered what would happen if I was in a meeting and it was time for me to do an ACIM lesson.

"Relax," my newly wiser self-said. "Stay present."

Another one of my concerns was the possibility that I would revert to my more maniacal Type A work personality. Would I be able to incorporate the more centered, clear, present, and compassionate Michael I felt I'd come to be while making money at the same time?

Just before Christmas 1990, and after a two and one-half hour interview in their San Francisco office, I received an offer from ABT.

I found an apartment in San Francisco, bought some basic living and household items like silverware, pots, and pans, and cleaning stuff, and a bed. I got my artwork and clothes out of storage, but I didn't buy additional furniture, as I didn't know how long this job would last or how I would like it.

Part of my job would be to teach clients, most of the large corporations, how to use and implement project scheduling software in their daily planning and reporting. I would also be teaching them some basic project management courses that ABT had developed. Although I had never taught formal software classes, I had experience in standing up in front of people in a teaching environment.

My first duty was to learn ABT's Project Workbench software thoroughly. Because I had used an earlier version of the software at another company, I felt confident that I would quickly absorb the new features. This project management software was straightforward. The only difficult new function for me to understand and explain would be an updated automated scheduling feature.

For the first couple of weeks on the job, I sat at home each day and worked with the software to deepen my knowledge of its capabilities and learn how to use it. At the same time, I kept up with my ACIM lessons, creating a nice rhythm to my daily schedule.

Shortly after the third week, I got my first call to teach a client's team the two-day Project Workbench course. If it went well, ABT would get additional business from this client. I was a little nervous about it even though I'd walked through the entire course more than 20 times and had put in notes into my teacher's manual where I was going to incorporate my own stories about using the tool. I knew that by making some of my teaching personal, the students would be able to better relate to me and the product.

As I started working with client companies, I noticed a strong defensiveness within me. This defensiveness would arise when a client staff member would start telling me about what doesn't work in the tool or what they don't like about the software. I noticed myself react as if the tools' weaknesses reflected on me.

I knew I was capable of being defensive, but what surprised me was how, at times, I felt the need to defend my company's software design. My urge to justify the software's qualities became especially intense when my company came out with its "Windows" version. The year was 1991 and DOS (Disk Operating Systems) computer programs were fading from existence, and Windows versions were becoming the norm.

When a student pointedly told me that our product wasn't following "Windows standards," I felt that it was my job to defend my company. It was like my being in the Army. Back then I justified my behavior and actions as a government employee, although I didn't believe in what I was doing; here I was defending and justifying my company's programming and product choices unnecessarily. Now, just as before, the "Power is defensivelessness" statement came to mind. There was something for me to learn here.

The odd juxtaposition of my natural defensiveness and my ACIM lessons made for a life beset with conflicting emotions. I would get upset at myself for responding vehemently to a student's questions about my company's software.

To my relief, the feedback about my software courses was very positive, especially about my ability to demonstrate how the software worked. There were always a few comments, however, that my intensity or tone was too pointed, even sometimes demeaning. These comment sheets would go back to my manager, and we would discuss them.

My meditation and ACIM practice had enabled me to accept these comments with equanimity and as opportunities to learn about myself. I'd gained a level of awareness that allowed me to see the feedback as my curriculum. I was starting to understand that I was in a school of sorts, a spiritual school that was laying before me my life's curriculum, the stuff I came into this life to learn.

All of us have our curricula, and each of us can each find ours by looking within.

For me, discovering my curriculum meant disconnecting my identity from the company I was working for. I could not go on believing that I was entirely responsible for the software and its components. I needed to accept that the software wasn't perfect, that the clients weren't always right, and that I wasn't always right. Letting go of my compulsion to have all the answers allowed me to interact more easily with my clients, so I'd have more opportunities to learn about both the software and myself. Most of all, I wouldn't be so defensive. This learning was a big step forward in my journey toward freedom. I was letting go of my need to be right.

As time went by, more and more of my work centered around teaching classes and mentoring clients one-on-one. Teaching others, I discovered, was an excellent opportunity to practice being present. It was mainly the case during group classroom teaching, which pushed me to grow. I began to acknowledge my students that I was there to learn as well and that I expected to learn something new during each class. My new openness inspired me to take more risks, and I began to cover the required material in different and unconventional ways.

I became unafraid of not knowing answers to questions. I could tell students I would research what I didn't know and get back to them. In classes where it was apparent that the students were there only because, as they said, "Our managers said we had to be here," I acknowledged their resistance. I told them I understood it and promised that I'd do my best to highlight the benefits of using the software so that they could see why their managers saw the software as valuable for them to learn.

Despite my learning how to deal with their attitudes, the going wasn't always easy. There were times when someone would say or do something that would send me spiraling into a defensive or arrogant mode of communication. Still, I was happy with the progress I'd made in letting go of my identity as the expert and in becoming more open in my interactions with people. When I could be open and transparent, most of the time, I could make amends to the person I might have offended or to the whole class.

During one two-day course for a major grocery store chain, for example, a student insisted on questioning everything I said, from the reasons for his company choosing the software to most of the aspects of how the software worked. With every chapter we covered, this individual's barrage of questions and negative statements took over the class and cast a negative pall over the classroom. At the end of the first day, one of the other students came up to me and said, "He acts this way all the time, so don't take it personally." I laughed and said, "Thank you," and told the student that I'd run into this kind of thing before and was comfortable dealing with it.

At the end of the second day, while everyone was dropping off their evaluation forms, the antagonistic student came up and said, "I must compliment you on not getting wrapped up in my negative remarks. It is the first time I've not been able to rattle a vendor teacher." I laughed out loud and thanked him for acknowledging his negativity in the class and for giving me an opportunity to continue my work on becoming less defensive and achieving a more composed identity.

Chapter 15

Non-Self - My Second Principle of Freedom

Instructing clients in new software and project management concepts and techniques were also teaching me about my curriculum and about how I responded to criticism.

To process this new information, during the evenings and on the days I was at home, I read my *Course in Miracles* text, other mind-opening writings, and meditated. This practice, together with my recent experiences in the work world, was broadening my understanding of the freedom I was seeking.

One of the core pieces of information that kept arising was the idea of "self" and my identification with this self. I saw that when I could step aside from the concept that there is a "self," my work life and my whole life felt more relaxed and free of deliberate encumbrances. Holding on to the idea of self, enabled to see that it's more difficult to be free when I associate myself with an identity or identities. It is like having to live up to an ideal or concept of who I was.

What I was learning was that if I allowed myself to be attached to an identity of self, that is, a particular image of myself, then I wouldn't be able to experience freedom. To achieve freedom, I would also need to let go of my desire to identify with something outside myself, or even in a set of beliefs such as those outlined in the *Course in Miracles*.

I don't mean to say that we can't learn from others' actions or behaviors, or from other teachers. It's when we follow mindlessly in someone's footsteps or identify with the belief that there is a self, we lose our freedom. The journey toward freedom is the journey of not holding on to a perception of self.

My new life was teaching me to let go of my perceptions of my nature and my self as a permanent, discrete entity. So, when I was teaching a software course, there would be nothing else I would be doing or thinking or planning for, no "self" separate from the teaching; I would be teaching the software course, doing nothing else. I would identify completely, solely, with what I was doing at that moment.

Who I think I am is just who I *think* I am, and at the same time, it is not who I am. Non-self, then, becomes my second principle of freedom:

Non-Identification
Freedom requires me not to identify with a "self" or hold on to ideas of what self is.

I've observed that we often make a tacit agreement with each other when we meet, especially for the first time. The agreement goes something like this: "I'll believe you are who you think and say you are if you believe I am who I think and say I am."

If I believe that I am strong, intelligent, defensive, beautiful, a planner, curious, thoughtful, quick-tempered, tall, stout, round-faced, strong-chinned, having large hands or whatever, I'm only sharing attributes and my ideas about who I think I am. Although I may have these attributes, are they really who I am? If I rely on these characteristics to define me, what happens when those things change? Do I quit being me?

We've all had the experience, and it is usually with old friends or family members, of their telling us something about how we believe about a subject we are discussing. Now we might have changed our opinion and belief around this subject since an earlier time. However, because the other person has held onto a perception of who we were, instead of who we are now, he or she misunderstands us. I have learned the hard way that if I've radically changed any beliefs, there are people who look at me very differently and sometimes with little acceptance.

This misperception also takes place when we don't accept the ever-evolving self. Not allowing our changing creates inner conflict. Being free means that your self is always changing and therefore the person you previously were, is not the self you are now. Thus, labeling any one thing or group of things as "self" becomes absurd. As we change, our inner labels will change, and we become some other version of our self.

Ram Dass put it perfectly: "Identifying with a thought or set of thoughts is a trap because as soon as you identify with a thought, another one will come along, then another, then another. So, which thought are you? Being caught in a flow of thoughts, you are not present with what is right in front of you." And what is in front of you is your life.

I remember a moment during my first 10-day meditation retreat in Yucca Valley in 1993 when I learned by direct experience how my illusory "self" could change from one extreme to the other in a brief moment.

During the first six days of the retreat, I regularly struggled with intense knee pain. Sometimes the pain would go on for an entire 45-minute sitting. At other times, the pain hit my knees in intermittent bursts during a session. Mentally, during these meditations, when I wasn't fighting the agony or trying to be at peace with it, I was spending my time planning. I kept thinking about how I was going to organize some future project management venture.

My tendency to lose focus on my meditation and plan things didn't surprise me because, after all, my project management/software teaching job was all about planning and teaching people how to prepare methodically. Even so, one reason I brought meditation into my life in the first place was to learn to be more present. Sporadically during these meditation sessions, I'd snap back to the present and realize what I'd been doing. Planning. I'd then tell myself non-judgmentally, "Planning. Now back to the breath."

That is how it went during the first six days. All I seemed to be doing was associating with my planning self and my knee-pain self. The behavior evolved into the criticizing person—I was someone who couldn't attend an extended retreat and was a lousy meditator. It seemed all I really wanted to do during this retreat was have some time to plan a future business event in between extreme bursts of knee pain.

For some reason, on the morning of the seventh day, I woke up and my mind seemed free of my planning encumbrance. It seemed more spacious and present with what I was doing at the moment. I also found myself not having any knee pain. Delighted, I felt relaxed and joyful during the sitting and walking meditations through the whole day. At one point, a thought arose that said; "I think I'm getting this." During that evening's dharma talk, I was feeling expanded and centered, and another thought came to me: "This is it. All I need to do is hold on to this expanded feeling of peace, presence, and equanimity and I'll be fine." And just as I started to use my mind to figure out how to hold on to this new "self" that I had become in that moment, the whole feeling collapsed. A raging and searing pain darted into the depths of my knee, and the peace and serenity that I had worked so hard to achieve precipitously bolted out of my body through the ceiling of the meditation hall and into the vast space beyond our solar system. I was limp, despondent, and crestfallen that I wasn't the beautiful, spacious, present person I had been just one moment earlier.

Most all of us, at some point, question our identity and existence. Many people ask the obvious question; "Who am I?" They answer the question by listing attributes they consider themselves to be. These attributes, however, are only descriptors of either the internal or external state of a person's being for that moment or of a pattern of behaviors. Because these attributes can and will change at any moment, we cannot use attributes to answer the question of who we are.

Two other age-old questions are still being debated: "What is consciousness?" and "Do we have a soul?" I do not claim to have the answers, but I would like to share some thinking on these subjects that might shed light on "the self."

In 1997, Time Magazine published an article on the subject of consciousness, self, and the soul. The author, Madeline Nash, reported on studies of consciousness, self, and what happens in the brain when people appear to be unconscious or have suffered strokes and seizures. In almost all cases their minds continued to show the same level of activity as those of people who are conscious. The measured brain activity of a conscious person and an unconscious person was the same, but the outward expressions of these subjects were significantly different.

In this article, Dr. Antonio Damasio, a Portuguese-American neuroscientist who has shown that emotions play a central role in social cognition, wrote that he "doesn't regard any one region of the brain—or the brain as a whole—as the seat of consciousness." Instead, Damasio sees the brain as an interconnected system with cognition and sensory processes centered in different areas. Consciousness, he says, is "similarly dispersed." He goes on to state that maybe consciousness "is the feeling of knowing that we have feelings." Damasio concludes that maybe Rutgers University's Colin McGinn had it right when he said, "A full understanding of consciousness and its origins—like that of life itself—will always elude us."

The answer to the second question, "Who are we?" becomes more evident when we free ourselves from the incarceration of a set identity. Only then do we discover, both with feeling and cognition, that we are not solid at all. Our physical body is always replacing itself molecule by molecule, and the universe around us is shifting moment by moment. Viewed in the present, we aren't our feelings or thoughts either, because these are fleeting as well.

Our sense of self is born soon after we are. Then our list of attributes that define us develops from experiences from childhood to adulthood. We further clarify these attributes when others judge us, and we learn from the world's standards to judge ourselves. Finally, we hone these attributes by inventing an idealized view of self in comparison to others. We are better than, worse than, or the same as somebody else.

The self that is crafted by opinion is not reliable. Not only is it dependent on the outside world (dependent origination), it can change in a moment, invalidating its very existence.

I'm not saying that we don't have a functional self that operates in the world, a person that knows how to use a computer, cook dinner, and solve a math problem. The concept of non-self, as taught in Buddhist teachings, means not equating these functional aspects and attributes of our self with the totality of who we are.

How can we free ourselves from the prison of a self-built set of opinions? One way is through inquiry. By examining each of the identities we find ourselves holding on to, we can see through to a more expansive sense of self, unencumbered by the values we've placed on a set of attributes. Meditation is an excellent tool for looking into our self-associations with roles that we misidentify as our self.

In her book *Loving What Is,* Byron Katie gives us four questions that we can ask ourselves about the truth of our assumptions:

- "Is this true?"
- "Can you absolutely know that it's true?"
- "How do you react, what happens, when you believe that thought?"
- "Who would you be without that thought?"

When I asked myself these questions, a spaciousness around my curriculum, my life path, opens around me. I'm suddenly open to more choices. Having additional choices is exhilarating and at the same time uncomfortable.

For example, I had been actively identifying with a specific role, "project manager." As vacation time approached, I found myself wanting to decide where I might go. Looking at it as a project to manage, I'd want to know the where, when, and dependencies of all my travel arrangements. Where will I sleep each night? Does it correspond with my travel? And food: How to explore the types of restaurants near each stop so that I could make a "better" (there's that picking-up-pieces-of-wood scenario again) hotel selection? Should I prioritize the needs for travel, food, and hotels to create a trip I could enjoy or on that at least met my expectations? When I freed myself from my identification with my role as project manager, I became more creative about deciding where I would spend my vacation and what I would do there. The possibilities of my trip exploded with options.

Freeing my self didn't mean forgetting my work role. It's about keeping it in perspective. Katie's lesson is that identifying deeply with a character limits our thoughts, feelings, ideas, and actions; it limits possibilities.

Most of us spend a lot of our time living in a state of self-consciousness. By self-consciousness, I don't mean embarrassment or nervousness. Instead, I mean our orbiting attention on who we are at the moment. By inquiring deeply through meditation, we may come to a point where that recitation begins to disintegrate and fall away. The circular thoughts quit coming back at us, and we can experience not knowing who we are. Our self-consciousness, for a moment, is gone.

When this happens, it can be frightening at first. Most of us need the security of knowing where and who we think we are at any given moment. During meditation, we can travel closer to losing our sense of self. We are always free to pull back when we touch our fear of dissolving into emptiness.

Paradoxically, the journey to no-self calls for us to start with a strong sense of self. As Ram Dass wrote: "…you may have to become somebody to become nobody." That is, if we try to surrender our judgment-built identity prematurely, we will keep returning to that sense of self because fear can and will arise if we lose our sense of self before we develop a trust of non-self.

When our self-identity is weak, we will at first equate losing self-consciousness, or awareness of ego, with losing ourselves entirely. Self and the ego, however, will never be forgotten. They will merely lose their position of power. The self is always available and summoned at any moment, but it no longer calls the shots.

Our ego is a formidable challenge to awareness. Its role is to build a kind of fortress from which we can deal with the world in our way. In doing so, it also erects a wall between our public identity and the truth of who we are. Therefore, it stands to reason that losing ego tends to create fear of the unknown. We fear that loss as if it were a sort of death. We fear the end of our separate self. Not only that, we fear that we will lose our distinct identity and will no longer be recognizable to our self and others. We imagine that a non-self will feel like emptiness or nonexistence. This fear can be overwhelming.

But when we enter the state of freedom from self, we are amazed to discover that we are comfortable and happy. We realize that the person we left behind—the one we thought existed—doesn't, and was never really there.

The path of learning about our real existence is through the door of nonexistence, our separate nonexistence. We and the world we live in are filled with endless numbers of distractions that keep us from embracing our truth. Each of these distractions is a manifestation of our belief in our ego.

Chapter 16

Attachment, Aversion, Inquiry, & Integration

By the Fall of 1992, I had long finished reading *A Course in Miracles,* and its teachings had melded well with my ever-growing meditation practice. ACIM was indeed a mind-opening book. I had not only connected with its words, but I also felt a connectedness with them; I knew they spoke a truth from which I could continue my quest for freedom. I distilled my insights from ACIM into three short sentences: Love is real. Everything else is an illusion. Live in this realm, and you'll be at peace.

In practice, this meant not becoming attached to things outside myself and detaching myself from my internal thoughts, feelings, and preferences.

From 1992 to 1996, my job as a software consultant required me to spend a lot of time on the road at client sites. As I traveled, I found it easy to keep up with my daily meditations by being clear about my overall objective of having personal, internal freedom. Airplanes, it turned out, were great places to sit in meditation. They are mostly free from distractions; they kept me confined to one spot for as long as five hours; they were perfect places to close my eyes and breathe. Sitting in an airplane now was a far cry from the white-knuckle flying I'd been doing ten years earlier when fear of dying preoccupied my mind.

For two to three months at a time, my schedule had me flying into the same city, leaving each Sunday afternoon or evening and often coming home late on the following Friday night. After I completed the assigned contract, I would find myself at home for a week or two. Then I'd be given a new deal, and I'd travel to a new city and client site for a few months.

I didn't mind this schedule. Traveling to client sites also gave me the option to spend weekends exploring client cities on my own. When I stayed over on weekends, the clients benefitted because it cost them less to pay for my hotel than to pay for flights to and from San Francisco. In this way, I got to know Vancouver, Winnipeg, New York City, Chicago, Seattle, Salt Lake City, Boston, Austin, Portland, Orlando, San Antonio, Calgary, Juneau, and other beautiful and interesting cities.

I was working happily in this job when I re-discovered the thriving meditation community in Marin County, the picturesque stretch of hills and small towns at the northern end of the Golden Gate Bridge. Spirit Rock Meditation Center had grown from the teaching of Jack Kornfield, a charismatic teacher with whom I had occasionally meditated on Monday nights in a local, Fairfax, California church.

That Monday night sitting group had grown considerably, and a group of devotees raised enough money to buy a beautiful piece of land in the Marin County town of Woodacre and named it Spirit Rock after the Native American name for a prominent rock outcropping on the land. In 1990 Spirit Rock opened a temporary meditation hall, and it was here that Jack's Monday night group sat together. I began to join them when I wasn't traveling.

Now that my new life was supplying my basic needs, and because meditation was a growing part of that life, I wanted to get more involved with this beautiful place. My involvement became three-fold. I sat as a student. I volunteered my time by working on the land. I contributed financially. In return for my contributions, I received a community of people I could relate with, and my daily practice grew stronger. My fellow student practitioners provided companionship, and the Spirit Rock teachers guided me. I felt the support of both, even while I sat in some city thousands of miles away.

Buddhist insight meditation as practiced at Spirit Rock felt very congruent with ACIM's lessons. Both counsel detachment from thoughts and the mind's perceptions of the physical world. The more I learned about Buddhist doctrine, the more I found synergy with what I was discovering to be correct about freedom. The Buddha's Four Noble Truths contain the essence of his philosophy. I'll summarize them:

1. **There is suffering.** Suffering comes from phenomena like physical pain, fear, or mental distress. It also exists because change is always present and therefore everything is transitory (i.e., life leads to death). We may, at any time, find ourselves suffering from any of these things. If we are motivated to seek fulfillment in what is temporary and susceptible—and it doesn't take much introspection to recognize how sensitive our feelings and bodies are—we will always suffer disappointment and a sense of loss.

2. **Desire and/or attachment causes suffering.** Longing for something or attachment to something is interpreted as wanting this something to be different from what it is. In seeking fulfillment from what is transient, we miss out on what is going on in our life. Attachment and aversion are the primary vehicles that drive us to seek gratification outside ourselves. Attachment is holding on to the things we want to keep in our life and resisting change. Aversion is wanting to push away the negative forces in our life.

3. **This suffering can end.** If we can let go of our conscious and unconscious self-centered habits of seeking fulfillment from what is

transient, we can meet life as it is, not as we think it ought to be, and our suffering can end.

4. **The Eightfold Path is a way to end suffering.** The Eightfold Path is Right thought, Right speech, Right action, Right livelihood, Right understanding, Right effort, Right mindfulness, and Right concentration. "Right" means they entail living in accordance with mindfulness, virtue, and wisdom. These are practical guidelines for living life, and as one follows them, there will be a natural movement towards freedom.

These truths are the core basis for Buddhist teachings. My own experiences with attachment and aversion have shown the second truth about the desire to be especially apt for me. Whenever I find myself wanting something to be different from what it is, I feel a pang of suffering.

Buddhist thought also identifies three types of responses to our experience of any internal or external stimuli; Pleasant, Unpleasant, and Neutral. The Buddha calls them the "Three Feeling Aggregates." The pleasant aggregate experience can easily cause us to develop an attachment, no matter if the stimulus is a thought, feeling, or object. The unpleasant aggregate experience can cause us to develop an aversion to the stimulus, whether it is a thought, feeling, or object. The neutral aggregate experience rarely affects us because we don't care about it and tend to ignore it.

It is, of course, inevitable that we become attached to pleasant aggregates and even unpleasant ones. The practice of meditation gives us an opportunity to step away from these attachments or aversions consciously as the mind wanders from pleasant to unpleasant thoughts and back again. The three aggregates were becoming an excellent tool for me to use in the process of being mindful of what I had in my life and, more importantly, why.

On my days off from work with ABT, I could be found at Spirit Rock, moving boulders in the creeks or clearing brush or making trails. When I could work it into my schedule, I sat daylong retreats during weekends and spent most of my non-working weeks attending longer retreats. By 1992, I started planning part of my vacation time to coincide with the springtime desert Yucca Valley Retreats that Spirit Rock held at the Institute of Mentalphysics in Joshua Tree, California. The spring retreats were terrific because I could sense an awakening in me during the time of year when nature is renewed. In the desert, the rebirth of spring is truly mystical.

It was during the first two Yucca Valley retreats that I began to break free from my preconceived view of "how" the world "should" be and grasped the profound power of non-attachment and non-aversion. I had come a long way since my first seminars with SAGE four years earlier. I was seeing and accepting things more as they were rather than what I wanted or perceived them to be. By 1995 and my third Yucca retreat, I was moving forward even more. I was now at home with the pace of my practice. I had learned that the changes from meditation would be slow, subtle, and grounded. It was time to change the outside aspects of my life, one by one.

During this time, late 1991-1995, my practice of meditation allowed me to pay closer attention to what was going on within my body. During meditation retreats, we were served plant-based meals, and I noticed what my body felt like after eating vegetarian food. It felt lighter, both physically and in spirit.

At home, I continued to eat meat, but in early 1992, after I'd had an unusually heavy meat-laden meal and disliked feeling heavy and sluggish the next day, I began experimenting with my food intake. By consciously noticing what I felt like when I did and didn't eat red meat, I saw changes and noticeable differences in how my body responded to activity and even how it smelled. As a result, I chose to stop eating red meat; I simply liked the results. Soon I started questioning my responses to chicken and fish, and before 1992 ended, I had dropped all types of meat from my diet.

Soon after, I made a second change in my lifestyle. I stopped watching television. This form of entertainment, like meat, made me feel sluggish after a few hours, not to mention that I was engaging in stuff that meant very little to me, things like game shows and sporting events involving teams with whom I had no links, plus sitcoms and other series-type programs that held little or no interest for me. Meditation and the three aggregates had sharpened my awareness of the influences around me, so I could now see that by sitting in front of the TV watching games, especially football, I was not engaging in the world. I was just numbly watching the action that meant very little to me. By the fall of 1992, I'd had it with this habit. Sitting in a Starbucks one day with an acquaintance, I casually asked him if he would like my TV. He said "Sure," so we got up, hopped into his van, and drove over to my house. I unplugged the TV and VCR, and we loaded them up. Since then, I've rarely missed having a TV set. If I'm near one, I can easily slip into watching. The difference from my old TV days is that I am capable of turning it off and I will. I can see how I'm spending my time and I can make a choice.

Changing my life was now becoming almost second nature to me. So far, I'd changed my eating habits and my TV watching habit. My next change would feel like a logical extension of those changes. My recent TV watching had gotten me thinking about changing my attitude about something that had been a significant factor in my life— competition. I'd started rethinking my attachment to competitiveness while I watched the televised sports I had been hooked on, and the crowds that cheered at these events. Watch the crowd at a hockey game during a fist fight on the ice. I was asking the question: Was my competitive spirit affecting me the way I saw it harm others? The more I asked myself, the more apparent it became that yes, both winning and losing created energy in my mind and ego that felt neither healthy nor peaceful.

My inquiry into my competitive nature brought about a new understanding of what it might have been like for others. What about the guys who were always chosen last when teams were selected on the playground? Did they feel like losers? My new understanding and compassion about how they might have felt led to further reflection on the concept of competition itself. It inevitably produces winners and losers. What does it feel like to be labeled as a loser? How do kids and adults who are often labeled losers deal with it? And how do the results of competition manifest broadly in our society?

My ruminations about competition were not well received by my friends and even a few of my fellow meditators. They argued that competition helps people excel, and if done mindfully it helps people learn about teamwork and good sportsmanship. Although I'd agree with the collaboration and good sportsmanship aspect, I don't necessarily believe that running faster, jumping higher, or throwing farther helps our society grow spiritually. I also think there are other, possibly better, ways to learn teamwork. What I was wondering about regarding competition, had more to do with its very existence. Why do we need to function in a world that labels some of us as losers and others as winners? Does excelling in some physical competition expand our planet's consciousness?

To be clear, I'm not saying that competition directly causes terrible behavior. The conclusion I drew was that competition is neither helpful nor necessary for developing teamwork, which can be taught in a non-competitive way. When competition leads to labeling people as losers or inadequate, it isn't helpful to the human spirit.

I decided that I would no longer participate in competitive events. I also steered away from competition for positions or promotions at work. I would do my job well and obtaining a promotion wouldn't be a goal. I won't compete for a spot. I had become detached from the desire for those rewards. Giving it up felt good and created a space of peace within me about work.

All told, I had now changed my diet, given away my television, and stopped basing my actions on competing with myself or others. These were only the more apparent transformations I'd made in my life because of my meditation. In a more profound sense, my willingness to change my life had been made possible by my willingness to become less attached to both the inner and outer things on which my life revolved.

At the beginning of this adventure, I was willing to give up one of my cars and most of my furniture, but it would have been safe to say that I still had a healthy attachment to what was "mine." As my meditation practice became a constant and healthy component in my life, I became less attached not only to what I owned but to the person I thought I was.

Another change that I underwent, subtle but no less profound, was a considerable increase in my generosity. In the past, I might have been generous with my money for special holidays and birthdays. Now I started giving money to different organizations whose ideas and ideals were either along the lines of mine or who promoted internal spiritual growth in a non-denominational way, such as Spirit Rock Meditation Center, Center for Attitudinal Healing which is based on the concepts of *A Course in Miracles*, Gaia House Meditation Center, and a couple of hospice agencies.

My new generosity also extended to family, friends, and strangers. I became generous with both my time and my money in the form of gifts and responses to requests for financial assistance. One recipient of my new generosity was a woman I befriended, whom I called "CR," a graduate student in psychology. CR had long, wavy, blond hair, bright, open eyes and a smile that went from San Francisco to New York, two places she had lived. She worked at a spiritual book and artifact store, Red Rose Gallery, on Chestnut Street in San Francisco. Whenever I would visit the store, she would be there. We would talk, and she would show me some of the new book releases that might interest me, or a new CD. In one of our conversations, she told me she was struggling with her boyfriend and her current living situation. She felt she needed some alone time to reduce the stress so that she could do her homework and write her dissertation in peace. Because I was generally away from my apartment five nights a week, I merely gave her a set of keys and told her to make herself at home while I was gone.

Giving someone a set of keys might not seem like a big deal for some people, but for me, it was a huge deal. I trusted my longtime friends to have unfettered access to my home, but I would not have imagined giving someone access I'd just met and only spoken with during visits to her place of work. Regardless of not having much stuff, I still felt very protective and attached to "my" stuff.

Having someone in my personal space also had a fun component. I like ice cream, and because I was gone so much, there was very little in my refrigerator except ice cream. I'd eat up to a pint a day. CR also liked ice cream. She would eat some of what I'd left in the freezer and replace it with a different flavor. So, before a trip, I'd place a pint of ice cream in the fridge and when I returned I would find a different-flavor pint in its place. We were treating each other to our favorite ice creams and learning fun things about our different tastes.

I was discovering, just about everywhere I looked, the real difference between having nice things and needing to have them. Appreciating or honoring something with little or no attachment is far different than having to have something to reflect on oneself.

Chapter 17

Detachment - My Third Principle of Freedom

When I returned from that Big Sur camping trip back in 1989, I got rid of most of my furniture. I didn't do it because I wasn't attached to my furniture; I was very connected. I got rid of my furniture and other belongings at that time because I had resolved to make a massive shift in my life and by discarding myself of possessions was one step in shedding the burdens of my past ways.

As a result, my San Francisco apartment was devoid of furniture. The bedroom had a bed, two nightstands, and a smoke-damaged chair I had rescued from a fire in San Francisco. The kitchen had an old fire-rescued table and a beat-up chair. A large closet off the living room held an inexpensive desk that I'd found at a garage sale. My only relatively valuable possession was a Concept II rowing machine that I had picked up after getting my job. It was the single object on the hardwood floor in the living room.

When my daughter came to stay, I would inflate a portable mattress and lay it down it in the living room alongside the rowing machine. This environment, I realized, was not very inviting for her. I also cared about providing a comfortable setting for visitors, so I decided to reverse my 'own less stuff' lifestyle and buy furniture. By then I was confident that I would not become overly attached to having stuff since the items themselves (furniture, cars, clothing) were never the real issue. It was my attachment to what those things represented that created my struggles.

I remembered that back in the 1980s I had placed tremendous importance on my things and would protect them robustly. I saw them as a significant part of my identity. When I bought a new car or even a used one, I was proud of it as seemed to validate my worth. I remember a CPA accountant friend of mine telling a story about one of his clients who had made a lot of money. "When I asked him how much he enjoyed his money, vacation home, cars, and a new boat," my friend said, "he smiled at me and said, 'what I've learned is that I don't own any of this stuff, it owns me.'" Now that I had relinquished my psychological dependency on having stuff, I could fully relate to this client's comment.

Many of us have relied on material items to define who we are. When we have that relationship with our stuff, we become unable to separate our identity from it. Often we make these attachments not only with external things but also with our ideas, concepts, and thoughts about ourselves and our relationship to the world.

My third principle of freedom is thereby

Detachment

Freedom requires me to be neither attached to nor strongly averse to things or experiences outside myself including the opinions of others about me, nor to ideas, attributes, and principles within myself.

This principle does not mean that I can't possess things that I like, appreciate, or even love. It doesn't say that I can't embrace ideas and concepts and enjoy my attributes. And it certainly does not mean that I can't learn from my experiences. Instead, it instructs me to notice when my decisions and choices are being adversely affected by an attachment or aversion to what I own or want, or to the sensations and feelings within myself. It is a reminder that they aren't synonymous with my identity.

The principle also pertains to my attachment to the people I love. I will naturally have deeper feelings towards them, which makes detachment more difficult. However, by being less attached to my feelings for them and their feelings for me, I can see them more fully as they are, not as my attachment wants them to be. Being detached does not mean not to love or care about those who are in our lives.

One day in January 1998 at the Spirit Rock Meditation Center, I applied the principle to my reflexive attachment to my favorite meditation teacher's guidance. I had been an active member of the Spirit Rock community for more than seven years. I was about to travel to England for my first 90-day silent retreat and had just finished a wonderful dinner in the Spirit Rock dining hall with my fellow yogis and teachers. Among them was Jack Kornfield, the teacher who had most influenced my meditation practice in recent years. The retreat I would be attending was the kind in which the participants sit and silently show up to themselves day after day. There wouldn't be any specific teacher, program, or sitting schedule to guide us. A non teacher-led retreat would be a new experience, so I thought I would ask Jack for some guidance beforehand. Pulling him aside in the crowded dining room, I told him of my plans to attend a 90-day retreat at Gaia House and wondered if he had any advice or guidance for me. He smiled that wry smile of his and said, *"Enjoy!"*

I had hoped for something a little more bounteous from Jack than the word *"Enjoy."* I mean, *"Enjoy"* is what someone might say to a friend going to Disneyland or Paris. I was especially disconcerted to get this sendoff from someone who averages at least one 45-minute Dharma talk a week and has been giving them for well over

20 years. I thought he would have had a little more to say, maybe some words of wisdom from his hundreds of written commentaries and notes. Wouldn't something in them be appropriate to my situation?

Over the nine years that I had sat with Jack at the Fairfax church and Spirit Rock, I'd observed that the notes he uses for his talks are handwritten, carefully stapled at the top of the page, and filled with highlighted text to identify quotes from an assortment of books and articles. Jack places these notes, books, and articles strategically in a half circle around him. While we sit in silence before his talk, he writes down new passages and thoughts as they occur to him so that the speech is as much in tune with his current views as possible. This system makes any statement by Jack relevant to what's happening at the moment he gives it. The resulting spontaneity makes them enjoyable and, at times, even mystical. Given his gift, I was hoping for, and attached to, getting that kind of wisdom from him now. I was eager to hear something personal to me, maybe even divine.

"*Enjoy?*" I repeated back with a touch of, 'is that all' quality to it.

"Yes," he said. "You know, you'll experience joys, sorrows, along with numerous ups and downs, just like a roller coaster, so what else are you going to do?" Now this was more like it, I thought, and for a brief moment, I believed he was going to launch right into a particular five-minute lesson tailored especially for me.

But his attention was pulled away into a conversation with another yogi seeking a thought or teaching. Although I did not get my five-minute lesson, Jack was probably right that I would experience all kinds of ups and downs and would end up having to choose to either *enjoy* or *not enjoy* the experience. Thinking of the word *enjoy*, as Jack spoke to this other yogi, I translated it into "in joy." I could choose to find joy in whatever came up. I could choose to be "in joy."

As I walked away, I realized I had learned three things from Jack's advice: One, I had an attachment to his giving me something special so I could pre-plan how I would embark on the upcoming experience. My lesson was to let go of my planning and merely be in the moment. Two, the number of words that convey advice doesn't always relate to the value of that advice. And three, how I work with this advice, not the information itself, is what matters.

Did Jack's counsel help me? Yes. The advice not only helped me to engage myself in the totality of the retreat but also gave me ways to engage with specific events during it. One example:

I had been sitting for just over 30 days when, after a particularly quiet and blissful sit, I got up to do walking meditation. As I made my way down the driveway toward a lane that meanders through the English countryside, I felt myself enter a stable state of open clarity; my senses attuned to the sounds of the wind and the birds chirping in the bushes. All at once, an overwhelming peace flooded through me, and I started to think "this is it."

Just as "this is it" passed through my being, I looked down to watch, in slow motion, my uplifted foot move forward and place itself over and on a dazzlingly beautiful, luminescent beetle. As the weight of my foot fell onto the back of this beautiful being, its exoskeleton was crushed and cracked open by the weight of my body—and there was nothing I could do to stop this event. The noise of the body crushing reverberated in my ears.

It was over in a flash. My awareness, my clarity, and my peaceful bliss collapsed as I crumbled to my knees in the middle of the driveway. Tears flowed down my face, and a sad, wailing moan reflected the mindlessness of my action. With shock, horror, and sorrow, I thought, "What have I done?" I stayed there crying over the crushed remains of the beetle for 15 minutes. Then I looked up and saw a car, engine idling, at the bottom of the driveway, patiently waiting for me to move. I lifted the remains of the beetle off the pavement with a stick and placed them in the neighboring field.

While my tears dried as I lay on my back in the field next to my crushed brother, I recalled Jack's advice, "*Enjoy.*" How could I be in joy after this mindless act? How is it possible to enjoy even being alive right now?

Then it dawned on me. I was filled with sadness because, first of all, I had killed a sentient being. And second, I was attached to my vision of the person I should be, in this case being mindful in my walking, and ended up not being—mindful.

I had hoped that I would learn to have more consideration about acts of killing after I killed people in Vietnam. Although the bug I'd just stepped on wasn't a person, it was a sentient being I had slain, and I'd done it mindlessly. I was now feeling deep compassion for this bug's life. Lying there looking up at the sky, I recalled that just a dozen years ago, I was someone who simply killed any bug that invaded my space. Whether it was a spider, fly, bee, or any insect that was where I deemed it didn't belong, I would kill it. Now, look at me, in deep sadness and mourning over one mindless act that resulted in the death of a beetle. This sadness, however, also pointed out that I now had compassion for a bug, and that was something I could embrace with joy. Smiling, I thought again of Jack's one-word advice.

Freedom requires maintaining a level of detachment from ideas about myself. I had just become attached to my perception that "this was it" and that I was moving into some enlightenment phase of my life, only to see the "self" I hoped I'd achieved fall to earth like Icarus. If I wasn't attached, I might have been able to view my walking with mindfulness and see the bug. Instead, because I was so caught up in my perception of myself, I forgot to pay attention to what was right in front of me, under my foot.

Holding on to our preconception of ourselves is like keeping life anchored down as if it were a boat in the sea while the tides of life change beyond us. Thus, attachment limits the range of responses we can make to any given situation. Whether we become attached to our idea of ourselves or things outside of ourselves, our attachment limits freedom.

Is it possible to have nice things and enjoy freedom at the same time? Yes, if our identities don't confuse the things with who we are. For me, learning this lesson increased my freedom to choose what I would and wouldn't bring into my life.

As I went about buying furniture for my new San Francisco apartment, the change in me from the last time I performed this task became evident. I was buying nice things, but my feelings for them stood out in stark contrast to my possessiveness of the stuff I sold after my Big Sur camping trip. Make no mistake. I loved my apartment and enjoyed the city skyline views from the bedroom and living room. It had a great open living room with beautiful hardwood floors occupied only by my rowing machine, and I wanted to decorate it in a way that suited my tastes, but I had to ensure myself that *not* having this stuff was great as well.

Helene F., from my SAGE days, was a part-time designer, and as a first step, she took me to the Furniture Mart in San Francisco. There I ordered a custom couch upholstered in a modern black on black fabric. I built on it with other striking furnishings such as a 10-foot by 12-foot rug, off-white with black and red arcs streaming from the corners to the middle.

I was excited to be creating a living space that I designed expressly for my tastes. Much of my taste for a modern look and feel came from my mother. She had become quite an excellent abstract-expressionist painter, and I loved and admired her work. I had stored a number of her paintings, and when I took them out of storage I took great pleasure in hanging them in arrangements that reflected my simple style. To my eyes, the result was stunning: The beautiful black-on-black patterned couch; black-on-black side chairs with curved black wood arms; clear glass tables with black metal legs; a massive palm with big green flowing fronds forming a canopy over the couch; a modern standing lamp behind the sofa that splashed yellow-white light up to the curved ceiling. Most striking of all, the couch-table-chair grouping sat on the beautiful rug, creamy white patterned with black and red. Behind the couch, in the bay window nook, I placed a small glass table with etched crossed lines that gave it the look of a chess board, and as accents, two gorgeous, modern Italian chairs with deep red leather seats.

The design was arresting. I liked it. I also was confident that if it were taken from me, I'd be just as happy living in an empty apartment. By not becoming attached to the furniture, I had achieved an ease with my ownership of it, freedom of sorts. As it turned out, a few years later, I realized I wasn't using my living room very much, and I sold all the furniture for about one-quarter of the original price. And never really missed it.

Therefore, desires don't necessarily have to be hindrances. Wishes can be helpful to our growth. For example, the desire to resolve unresolved pain, sorrow, or sadness in our lives and to mitigate anger is a positive attachment to our feelings. Wanting to be kinder and have more compassion towards others is a constructive desire to be embraced. However, when the desire (attachment or aversion) pushes me to go into areas where I'm making choices to feed my ego, self-worth, or sense of self-importance, then I need to inquire within to better understand the root of the desire and how it drives my behavior.

Consequently, it is critical for me first to discern whether they are hindering my freedom. How do I figure out if I've become attached to a particular desire? When I honestly examine my feelings, I can quickly identify a hope that is a hindrance. Truthfully probing my thoughts, behavior, and resulting actions, I can ask if this is the person I am. One useful tool for mitigating attachment or aversion is to ask ourselves Byron Katie's four questions from her book *The Work*. They're in Chapter 15 and again below.

Cars and Generosity

I have always liked cars, and I've owned a fair number of them. Of course, I understand now that at times my attachment to vehicles was a poor choice. For instance, in college, married, and with a child, I sold a reasonably new, reliable Datsun sedan to buy a two-seat Porsche 914-6. Not only did I have to work more hours to afford the car, but it was also impractical for taking my wife and daughter anywhere. But it was cool, drove fast, and gave the impression, I thought, that I was successful.

Cars have always been a part of my life. On my sixteenth birthday I got my driver's license, and the following day I bought a two-year-old vehicle on which I made payments for one year. Since then, I've always had an automobile, sometimes one that owned me as I worked to make payments and maintain the machine. I often associated my self-worth with the car I was driving.

In June 1996 I had started my management consulting business, partially to honor my father's entrepreneurial spirit and partly to broaden the reach of my well-regarded abilities as a large-scale IT systems development consultant and planner. In my six years of daily meditation practice, I had learned to be more mindful of my choices and actions. Now I found myself making what was, for me, a lot of money. Before this venture, my highest base salary was just over $96,000 per year and with bonuses, over $115,000 per year. Going into business for myself, I billed over $120.00 per hour for my work, and my client list kept me working full time. Minus my expenses, I was clearing well over $200,000 a year, new-found territory for me.

This new-found access to money prompted a new spirit of generosity and inspired me to give much of my money to non-profit organizations that needed it more than did. With my years of practice and the help of some extraordinary teachers, I thought I had achieved the freedom to give and the freedom to own. When it came to cars, however, I wasn't there yet.

I could blame the car, but that would not be honest. It was as if a switch inside me flipped my consciousness to unconsciousness. Before I knew it, I was obsessed with buying a cool set of wheels.

Oh, sure, there was a vestige of awareness alive inside me: I made an honest effort to ask myself what it was about buying an expensive new car that had me so jacked up. It became fun to watch my mind make up good reasons for me to have this car: My current car was getting old, had many miles, and I wasn't very comfortable driving to and from Sacramento every week for work. It didn't have enough lumbar support, so my back hurt during the drive. And so on.

I'd done my homework, and my ego had decided on a new BMW 5 series. I visualized myself driving around in it, and I found myself thinking that I must be successful and that others might see me this way as well. I could feel my ego swell, but I kept justifying my decision based on how much my back hurt and how well a new car would fix this.

One Friday afternoon, while driving home to San Francisco from Sacramento, I realized just how obsessed I was with the idea of getting the BMW, and I came up with a unique way to begin the process of letting go of the obsession. Asking myself Byron Katie's four questions, I got these answers.

- **Question 1: "Is this true?"**

   Answer: Would my back feel any better and would I be more successful if I had a new car? The solution was yes, maybe my back might feel better in a new car because it would have more modern seats and the new car would have better lumbar support. Would I be more successful? No, the car would only be a manifestation of the success.

- **Question 2: "Can you absolutely know that it's true?"**

   Answer: "Maybe" was the operative word in Answer 1. I don't know if the lumbar support in the new car would help my back. One way of finding out would be to purchase a supportive lumbar pillow which would save me at least $55,000. My financial success wouldn't change whether or not I had a new car. Depreciation would make the car less valuable. Therefore, I didn't have to buy a new automobile to help my back. The truth was that I wanted people to see me as successful and I wanted to be seen from the outside as successful. It was all ego.

- **Question 3: "How do you react, what happens, when you believe that thought?"**

  Answer: If I believed that myself and others would perceive me as more successful with a new car, then I'd always have to buy a new car every year. And why limit it to cars? Why not buy other things that would represent my new-found success? And how can "things" that I acquire mark my success? The truth is, they can't.

- **Question 4: "Who would you be without that thought?"**

  Answer: I would certainly have more money if I didn't buy the car. I'd be just as successful while not needing to have my ego display this success. And if I were willing to let go of an attachment, it would make no difference if I had the car or not.

Even after coming up with these answers, I realized that I wanted to figure out a way to desensitize myself to the looks of the car to assist in changing my attitude towards buying it. To this end, I downloaded a picture of the car and made it the background desktop picture on my computer.

Day after day, I looked at the car in all its glory. Then, after six months, I noticed that I was becoming tired of the image and with it, the need to have the car. The obsession was dying, and the attachment to having the car was ending. It was like having an out-breath and being able to relax away from the idea of a new car. It was becoming comparable to my relationship with my furniture: It's nice, it reflects my tastes, and I can live with it or without it.

With this newfound inner freedom, knowing I could have the car or not have it, one Saturday I drove down to the dealer, test drove it and leased it.

I did find that people looked at me differently after I leased the car. My clients enjoyed teasing me about having a nice car, for which they were paying. Some of my friends looked at me with a slightly different attitude. They also knew that I worked hard and deserved to reward myself for my hard work.

In the end, I knew that I had leased the car free of attachment. If circumstances changed, I was confident that I wouldn't force myself to work to keep it. Less than a year later, I had an opportunity to take some extended time off, participate in an extended meditation retreat, and travel for six months. I had no trouble ending the lease and absorbing a financial loss with no remorse. I was free to begin a new chapter.

The power of non-attachment allowed me to enjoy something beautiful, and when circumstances shifted, it allowed me to take another step with freedom and peace.

Chapter 18

Letting Go - My Fourth Principle of Freedom

Inspecting my first three principles—Forgiveness, Non-self, and Detachment—I realized there was an arising theme behind them: learning to let go. This term is often used, sometimes flippantly, to tell someone to move forward from a situation. What it doesn't include is…how. How does one let go? These definitions and processes have worked for me:

- To let go does not mean to stop caring **about** something or someone else. It is the realization that no one can care **for** another person. Each person is responsible for his or her feelings. Attempting to care **for** someone would mean trying to take responsibility for their feelings. Caring for someone else cannot be done.

- To let go does not mean to change or blame another person. You and I can change only ourselves.

- To let go is not to attempt to fix another person but to support that person's attempts to change. Each person has to find their way—support this.

- To let go is not to do **for** another person but to let her or him learn from naturally occurring consequences. It means that I can support others in affecting their outcome.

- To let go is not to dwell on past events but to make mindful choices now.

- To let go is not to dwell on future events but to make mindful choices during present events, to understand that the future does not exist. (When you do this, the future will take care of itself and become the present you are in.)

- To let go is not to judge or criticize another but to continue to move toward accepting that person as he or she is.

- To let go is not to nag, scold, or argue about someone else's shortcomings but to correct my weaknesses.

- To let go is not to protect someone from reality but to support their facing and to engage with reality.

- To let go is not to adjust everything to my desires, but to receive, accept, and embrace each day as it is.

- To let go is to not see things as problems but to see them as opportunities to change.

- To let go is not to embrace terror but to see the uncertainties of life as adventures.

- To let go is not to move or act from a place of ambition but to act and move from a place of inspiration.

- To let go is not to sell people on something with the goal of getting something in return but to provide a service and accept the received results.

- To let go is not to act from fear but to act from love.

Surely you've heard these instructions on how to catch a monkey. Take a wooden box and cut a hole just big enough to slip an apple or an orange inside. A monkey that wants the fruit will reach in, grab it, and attempt to pull it out of the box. But it can't because holding the fruit makes its hand too big for the hole. It's a rare monkey that will let go of the fruit to escape.

A human who will not let go of a previous act or event is trapped just like the monkey. Holding on to how we were wronged, what we could have done differently, or the pain and sorrow of an event, keep us trapped in the past.

Another ancient story concerns two monks who are walking from their home monastery to another temple 10 miles away to attend a Buddhist celebration:

These monks came from a monastery that had numerous precepts, one of which was that they were not to engage with females in any way. They had not gone far when they heard, from a distance, what sounded like a woman's voice. As they proceeded down the trail, they listened to this voice more and more clearly, and it seemed like a plea for help. When the path reached a swiftly flowing river, they found the owner of the voice calling out for assistance—a woman far too small to cross the river safely by herself.

As the monks approached, she rushed up and asked them to help her. She desperately needed to cross the river because her children and husband were in a little village on the other side. The monks looked at each other, then turned back to her. One of them said, "We are sorry, but we cannot assist you. We have taken vows never to touch a female, and to break this vow would be strongly frowned upon by our abbot." The woman explained her predicament again. "My children are young. Their father needs to leave the village to find work, and they cannot be left alone. I need to get home as quickly as possible. Won't you please help me cross the river?" Turning back and facing each other, the monks reminded themselves to not break their vows.

As they conferred, however, one of the monks decided that helping this woman get back to her family was important, and he decided to break his vow and carry her across the rushing water. The other monk was extremely upset. He protested. He muttered loudly. He stepped carefully from stone to stone as his companion made his way across the river carrying the woman on his back. When they reached the other side, the monk carrying the woman stopped and gently let her slide off his back. She thanked him profusely and vowed that she would always provide support to the monks' monastery. The monks bowed, turned, and resumed their journey.

About five miles down the road, the monk that had not carried the woman continued to mutter and fume out loud about what his companion had done. Finally, he stopped, faced the other monk, and said, "You know that touching and carrying that woman across the river was against our vows and yet you did it anyway. I'm ashamed that you dishonored yourself, our vows, and our monastery." His companion looked him straight in the eye and said, "I am aware that I broke that vow. However, I just carried her across the river and then let go of that act. I see that you have been carrying her ever since."

This story sums up my fourth principle of freedom.

Letting Go

Freedom requires me to let go of past events and actions. It does not mean that I forget the lessons I learned from those actions or events. Letting go means, I release and let go of the past and pay attention to the now.

Jack Kornfield's book *Bringing Home the Dharma* quotes his teacher Ajahn Chah: "But freedom comes directly from letting go. If you let go a little, you will have a little freedom. If you let go a lot, you will have a lot of freedom. And if you let go completely, your heart will be completely free."

Letting go allows us to move on and to not be stuck in the past. It also enables us to to be free of want or wish. One example of letting go came my way on a Sunday morning, October 29, 1995, at 1:16 a.m. in Morro Bay, California. That morning I once again learned what it meant to be present, breathe, let go, and say "thank you."

My father had been ill for many years with heart problems. In the previous two years, he was also treated for malignant tumors in his brain and his lungs. Although chemotherapy and radiation treatments had left him weak, bald, and at times despondent, they did their job by arresting the cancers. The tumors weren't dead and gone, just in jail for the time being. If the cancer cells could be held at bay, the doctors bet that he would succumb to the less painful death of heart failure.

I had flown down to Morro Bay for a visit with him this weekend, as I had done every couple of weeks over the last year. During my visitations, Saturday nights included a wonderful family dinner. My brother, his wife, and their two boys would join us for food and lively conversation. It was a carryover from my high school days when my friends would join us for dinner and opinions would fly back and forth across the table like the Blue Angels.

Back when I was in high school, my friends would come because the food was excellent and we could each have a beer and smoke cigarettes. Sometimes my dad would tell a tall tale about his abalone diving exploits off Portuguese Bend, or how he and Frank Shultz built a 32-foot cabin cruiser in our driveway, or how he rode his Harley Davidson into a brick wall with a girl on the back. About that story, he smiled devilishly and said, "Heh heh heh, no one got hurt, but I felt horrible bringing the girl back to her house and having to tell her mother about the accident. You see, she was forbidden to ride on the back of my bike." We would laugh and ask him to tell us another story. Usually, the motorcycle stories would stop with, "That all ended when I met your mom." My father would go on to describe meeting my mother. "She said to me, 'If you're going to date me you have to have a car because I won't ride on the back of that thing.'" Again, we would laugh, then my mom would try to change the story by saying something like, "I never said that. I just thought those things were dangerous. Does anyone else want some more potatoes?"

As the years went by and especially on this night, like any other Saturday night feast in the last year or so, it was my brother and me who were telling the stories. Some of them my parents heard for the first time. Like the time, at age 15, I took my mother's baby-blue Triumph TR3 out for a Wednesday night spin because my parents were at the theater. My brother was sworn to secrecy because he knew he would die by my hands if he told on me. As the story unfolded about that night, I spoke of how I gunned the engine while sharply turning a corner and hitting some water in a shallow ditch. "Yeah," I explained, "all I remember seeing was trash cans, garage doors, parked cars, and lights shining everywhere. It felt like I was on a tilt-a-whirl ride at an amusement park. When the car finally stopped spinning, I almost shit my pants." My brother's young boys, my nephews, roared with laughter, and my mother looked at me incredulously and said, "I didn't know you stole our car."

"Yeah," my brother chimed in, "he did it lots of times and even took me out on a couple of occasions." My parents just shook their heads in disbelief.

This night, after a delicious dinner of lasagna, garlic bread, broccoli, and salad, Dad mentioned that he wanted to watch the World Series, so we all moved into the living room with our pie, coffee, and water.

In the past few months, Dad hadn't spoken much. He usually would sit and listen. I had noticed a slow peace taking over his life. It was almost as if life had finally wrestled him to the ground and made him say "uncle." Now as life was sitting on his chest, pinning him down for the last time, he seemed to be looking up and saying, "Hell, this ain't a half bad view from down here." In this peace, there was also his ability to listen a little more. I knew he was intently listening and drinking in the words and stories of his family, the family he would be soon leaving.

At about 9:30 PM, he told us he was going to bed. We all hugged him and said "Good night." I remember kissing him on his forehead and saying "I love you" as he slowly shuffled hunch-backed out to the back patio and had his nightly cigarette before going to bed. After he came back into the house, Mom followed him to the bedroom to tuck him in. When she came back out, she said, "Your father told me to reset the clock in the guest room. He wants to make sure you know the right time in the morning." He had been listening to my brother, and I talk about my Sunday morning flight back to San Francisco and wanted to make sure I didn't miss it.

After my brother and his family left, Mom and I stayed up talking and watching a movie until about midnight; then we decided to go to bed. I had just laid down after a short meditation in which I had asked the universe to allow me to be with him as he died when my mother knocked on the door. She looked distraught. "Dad is making funny breathing noises," she said, "and I can't wake him up." I pulled on some shorts and rushed to their bed. He was semi-conscious, his breathing challenging.

He opened his eyes just a bit and focused for a second, then lost focus. His breathing was arduous and noisy. I looked back up at Mom. She was lost, needing to hold on to something real, a thought, a duty, a task. She blurted out, "Should I call 911?"

I said, "Yes, but tell them there is no need to come with sirens. Then get dressed." I thought we might be on another trip to the hospital. She left the room to use the phone in the kitchen. I looked at Dad and said, "Stay here." But no sooner did those words tumble out of my mouth that it hit me: Looking at him, hearing his breathing, and sensing something very different, I realized this was it. He would be passing on. With this realization, I said, "Let it go, and I'll go with you as far as I can." I said this for both of us. I realized that if I could let him go, he could also let go. His eyes opened and focused on me for a moment, and then with a slight peaceful grin, his eyes shut.

With his head in my lap, I started to rub his back while holding his hand. I began to mimic and model his breathing. Together we breathed in and out. On the out breath, I would say, "Let it go. We love you. Thank you for being with us." After about five minutes of this, Mom came in dressed, ready to leave, and said, "How is he doing?"

"Not much better," I said, "He seems unconscious now."

"I called 911, and they're on their way," she said. "Should I call your brother?"

"Yes," I said. "Forrest needs to be aware of what is going on." She left the room to call Forrest and then went to wait for the paramedics to arrive.

I again focused on mirroring Dad's labored breath. After about two minutes, I knew he wouldn't see any more hospitals. He'd be gone in a matter of minutes. I kept hoping the paramedics were taking their time. I continued to breathe with him while thanking him for being my dad, for being Mom's husband, for being my brother's dad, for being a grandfather to my daughter and my brother's two boys. I thanked him for gracing our lives and the lives of everyone he contacted.

I continued to rub his back and breathe with him as his breath became more labored. There were a couple of shallow breaths, which seemed to be at 15-second intervals, then a couple more at 30-second intervals. I realized that it was becoming hard for me to mirror his breathing. With my inability so match his breath, I sensed he was letting go, I could feel him passing on, and I felt the room grow larger. Then all of a sudden, he had one big inhale with his eyes quickly opening all the way, a waiting period of what seemed like 10 to 15 seconds, and then a long slow full exhale with a slight rattle. I knew that I had witnessed his last breath.

As I sat there with a feeling of awe, it seemed that someone was filling the room with a soft, warm, liquid air clarifying and sharpening every detail. I was witnessing grace. It was the only word that seemed to be equal to the moment. Grace. It was the wholeness of living and dying in one fell swoop. It was the glory and peace of Love.

To this day, I can still touch the sensation of the grace I witnessed.

I am so very grateful for having learned the gift of letting go and how to be present to the moment at hand with equanimity and mindfulness. This gift, of being here now, allowed me to be fully present as a participant in the passing of my father's soul energy from one realm to another.

My dad's entrepreneurial spirit led him from time to time to start small companies or work in them. In 1979, he and I started a small convention cassette recording company called Sound Impressions, Inc. Because I'd been working at a small company called Audio Stats, recording convention seminars and workshops on audio cassettes and then duplicating and selling them on-site, I had experience in this business. The great thing about it is that I got to record some fantastic speakers such as Nobel Prize winner Linus Pauling, Rear Admiral Grace Hopper—who in 1952 wrote the first compiler for an electronic computer—Buckminster Fuller (inventor, author, system theorist and inventor of the geodesic dome), and Carl Rogers, whom some call the father of humanistic psychology. I got to spend one-on-one time with each of these renowned sages and had dinner with Pauling and Rogers. Recording these fantastic thinkers and my conversations with them was an honor and privilege.

I wasn't very good at selling, in contrast to my dad, who was one of the best, so he led that part of the business along with the financial end, while I went out and recorded and sold duplicated tapes.

Nine months after my dad passed and in honor of him, I decided to start my own company to offer clients services that I couldn't deliver as an employee of Applied Business Technology. With ABT, my job was to implement complex project management software systems for ABT's clients. However, my background in technology and management systems had given me the ability to provide clients with a broader range of services than ABT offered.

In June of 1996, I started my own consulting business, Tara Associates Inc. The name reflected my growing spiritual practice and referred to White Tara, who in Tibetan Buddhism, is known as the "mother of liberation" and who also represents success in work and achievements.

Chapter 19

Acceptance – My Fifth Principle of Freedom

I'm very familiar with anger. I have, on occasions, lashed out with a sharp, stinging tongue at strangers, friends, and family. I've hurt people with my words and have even gotten into a scrape or two because of my tongue.

From my work in SAGE, ACIM, and with curious inquiry during meditations, I've learned that anger has a deeper source. Anger, for me, is a secondary emotion, or as I like to think of the word "emotion," e-nergy in **motion.** Paying attention to myself and what is going on with me at the moment before my rising anger, I notice a feeling and that feeling source is almost always hurt, sorrow, or sadness.

When I looked deeper at my moments of anger, it's easy to see how times of being hurt have resulted in angry behavior. Often anger is the sensation and emotion I feel when I can't reconcile the way I think things ought to be with the way things are. Sorrow, sadness, or hurt often wells up inside when the world isn't being the way I want it to be.

Being cut off while driving can bring anger. Was the underlying feeling hurt, sadness, or sorrow because the person who cut you off didn't respect you and your space on the highway enough?

How about anger in a relationship? Could my anger be sorrow because my partner wasn't seeing me as a viable person?

How about in significant life events? If your child dies, could your anger at God be rooted in sadness?

Anger can have many different sources. By responding only on the surface level where all we see is anger with nothing behind it, we risk hurting others and ourselves even more.

What if we stop acting out from the emotion of anger and respond from the feeling of hurt, sorrow, or sadness? Would we react differently? What if we learn to accept the deeper feelings? How would we change?

Anis Nin once said, "We don't see things as they are; we see them as we are." Accepting our pain and our joy rather than fighting it can free us to see things as they are, and by doing so, we open our lives to the possibilities of freedom. We can use these emotions as tools to help us accept things as they are, not as we are.

The key is for us to recognize the triggers that cause our momentary ups and downs. Then we can exercise our free will and chose a different path if we wish to.

Acceptance, or seeing things as they are, is my fifth principle of freedom. It is the last one because we can reach acceptance only after we have embraced forgiveness, non-self, detachment, and letting go (release).

How can we tell when we're close to being able to accept things as they are? One positive sign is that we've stopped using the words "should" and "ought" to describe why we do not see things as they are. Should and ought are words we often use to tell ourselves how things could have been different from what they are and to place guilt, fault, shame or blame on the resulting what is.

To live in freedom means that we accept things the way they are, not necessarily as we want them to be, even when we are performing good works. The concept sounds far more unassuming than it is. Most of us know from our own experience that profound change is always more difficult to achieve than we imagined. The obstacle that we invariably run into is ego (the "self" we looked at in Chapter 15), which reminds us of how things *should* be. Our ego is a formidable foe of acceptance. It demands that we keep rearranging our world according to the ego's preconceived logic. Acceptance shows us freedom in the shining light of unvarnished truth. It is my fifth principle of freedom.

Acceptance

Freedom requires me to accept things as they are.

It requires stepping outside of myself to experience the moment without my thoughts and feelings being in the way. Acceptance does not mean condoning what is taking place. It says I merely observe how an event unfolds.

Acceptance also means viewing events with compassion and equanimity regardless of my personal beliefs.

Countless times in my life I have been unable or unwilling to accept things as they were. You've already read about a few of those instances of my wanting the world to exist as I wished it to be, not as it was. Refusing to accept reality was an unhealthy, let alone unhappy, way to live. When I learned to receive life's ups and downs, its stressful situations no longer got to me as much as they had. I saw what was happening and resolved not to be attached to a particular outcome. Even so, at times

I felt myself begin to resist what was going on, and my old frustration that the world did not march to my command would return.

Acceptance of what is: That is one of the most difficult challenges I know. However, by seeing and accepting things, people and events as they are, and not how we want them to be, our subsequent actions in these events or with people will become more mindful.

We all, at some level, view our seat in life to be the right view and others' views to be different and often inferior. All views are correct views given their vantage point. Are some people's opinions sometimes hard for others to embrace? Yes, and it doesn't make them less valid for the people who espouse those views.

The beliefs we stand by defining the borders of our understanding. When we surrender to acceptance, we gain a new power to see things as they are. Acceptance is thus essential to our ability to live in the realm of freedom.

How do we develop acceptance of things as they are?

In my case, I found acceptance when I developed the capacity to sense when I was casting blame, was clinging to an object or belief, or was rewriting the truth. I'm not always able to tag every ego-based act I commit, and that's okay. My five principles of freedom are not actions but a life-long practice that has no final goal.

Here are some of the tools that have helped to keep me on the path to finding acceptance.

Meditation

I use meditation almost daily to quiet my mind. By calming my mind, I give myself an opportunity to inquire and see what is impeding my understanding of the truth of things as they are. I stay open to discovering that I may not have behaved in accordance with freedom. The act of sitting in silence then serves as a base from which to examine truth and freedom.

For example, if I notice my ego is acting self-important—if, say, I'm blaming someone for something—quieting my mind through meditation gives me the perspective to look for a belief behind that blame that I can let go of. One of my pitfalls, I've discovered, is getting attached to the way I think things ought to be and then, if they don't work out that way, becoming disappointed in myself. When an event comes up during meditation, I have an opportunity to systematically look deeper into the origin of this disappointment, which usually turns out to be hurt, sorrow, or sadness.

Meditation has inspired me to find additional resources for deepening my insight into myself.

Therapists

A good therapist can be very helpful with the process of inquiry and reflection. As with anything else, however, it is essential to do your homework and determine if a particular therapist is a fit for you.

I have found that therapists who employ a bag of different tools, rather than just one technique can provide excellent support for discovering your path to truth. My goal with any therapist has been to gain an objective view of the events of my life, the feelings I have towards those events, and where they might have originated.

Examining one's past with a therapist can help develop empathy toward ourselves and others. This practice is especially useful for discovering opportunities for forgiveness. Good therapists also help us understand why we are where we are today. But therapists cannot by themselves transport us to acceptance. Even when we comprehend our past, we still have to take our steps to become free of our behavioristic drivers.

Seminars

Then there are seminars and workshops such as the ones I have described. A freedom seeker needs to consider whether a given self-help organization might be more about the egos of its leaders than about serving its participants. I learned amazing things about myself through my experience in SAGE workshops, but I maintained some distance from the organization's hype. Given the involvement, I loved my work with SAGE. Just because something isn't a perfect fit doesn't mean it can't be helpful.

Another example of an imperfect workshop from which I derived value is my experience with est (Erhard Seminars Training). I took a course in 1982, in Monterey, California, and I recall disliking the leaders and the severe, rigid protocols of the workshop. The value came from the tools it provided for taking responsibility for one's actions and one's life. The information and realizations were powerful. One of my favorite sayings came from est: "Ride the horse in the direction it's going."

Reading

Reading is an excellent way to begin to find what is right, or correct, for you. You'll see a list of books I've found helpful at the end of this book.

Many of my favorites are reflections of ancient texts and stories of a person's journey to discovery. I had to read some books more than once to appreciate them, such as *Heartwood of the Bodhi Tree*. I read this book a second time when my meditation practice was deepening, and I came to more fully understand and appreciate the depth of its message.

Most of the books on my list have been helpful on some level. *A Course in Miracles*, for example, gave me an opportunity to learn more about forgiveness and acceptance. Other books have merely opened my eyes to new concepts.

Acceptance of the Truth

Learning to accept the truth that is unattached to my ego isn't easy. I believe that the truth comes to each of us sometime in our life, even if it is during our transition from this life.

Reaching acceptance doesn't apply only to individuals. As science and scientists have made clear through measurable facts, the entire human species has reached a critical point at which all of us are facing some hard-to-face truths. Several factors, including climate changes, pollution, and widening economic gaps between rich and poor suggest that humanity's survival depends on our ability to evolve to a more conscious, less ego-driven state of being. I do believe that if all of us, or at least a significant number of us, begin to live and act in the truth of what is instead of what our ego-driven mentality wants, we won't have to witness our ultimate global truth—a transition on Earth that the human species might not survive. We will need to live in a spirit of oneness.

Humans, singly and collectively, can accomplish extraordinary things when we are focused to see and are willing to change what is. Fortunately, we have a long history of changing when we are on a precipice of crisis. In our present situation, waiting until we reach the precipice could make any action we take too late. Think of the difference between turning a 15-foot boat and a supertanker 1,503 feet long. The small vessel can change directions in a few feet. The supertanker requires miles. Do we have enough sea room ahead of us?

In the face of a pending crisis, many of us understand the danger and want to change, not only individually, but as a group and as a species. I sympathize with the urge to point at others and tell them, "You must change." First, though, as with everything else I've learned, each of us must first change ourselves. With enough people summoning the courage to make their changes, a tipping point is reached, and our species will evolve. Any variation on that scale, though, must come from within each of us.

Chapter 20

Taking My Seat

In December 1997, I completed a 20-month-long consultation with the State of California, and without any new client contracts in the near immediate future, I decided I would take some time off, attend an extended meditation retreat, and re-evaluate my future.

I looked at attending a structured, teacher-led, 90-day retreat at Insight Meditation Society (IMS) in Barre, Massachusetts, as well as retreats in India, Thailand, and Findhorn Center in Scotland. I also considered Vipassana Meditation retreats sponsored by S. N. Goenka which were offered in various locations around the world.

I had often wondered, however, if I could meditate on my own for extended periods. With that thought in mind, I became interested in a meditation center in the tiny village of West Ogwell, near Newton Abbot, three hours by train west of London. This center was founded by two excellent and insightful teachers,

Christopher Titmuss and Christina Feldman. Their center, Gaia House, was considered a sister center to both Insight Meditation Society and Spirit Rock Meditation Center. I had been active at both over the last eight years, even though Spirit Rock and Gaia House are 5,300 miles apart.

Between 1989 and 1996 I had attended two of Christopher's California retreats and had listened to several audio cassettes of his dharma talks. He was bright, engaging, and committed, and I appreciated his use of direct inquiry conversations with students during retreats as a tool toward understanding the truth. I had also attended a couple of short daylong retreats with Christina and felt connected with her energy, directness, and interpretation of the dharma. Besides the teachings and presence of its founders, Gaia House had a program wherein one could do a personal retreat.

This kind of retreat involved staying in your own room in the Hermitage Wing of the Gaia House center with a choice of either practicing and participating in the visiting teacher's group retreats or practicing alone in a specific meditation hall in the Hermitage wing that is reserved solely for sitting in silence uninterrupted by bells, teachers, or talks.

I found the thought of doing a meditation retreat, not being directly led by a teacher, both inviting and scary. In essence, the Gaia House program was offering me the opportunity to expand my meditation experience through my willingness and perseverance. Would I sit just the minimum amount of time required or would I develop my practice and sit expanded hours untiringly to see more clearly or even become enlightened at some level?

The questions I contemplated were: What was my level of commitment? Was I willing to move my sitting practice and understanding of personal freedom forward? I needed to answer this question honestly because I'd be spending the whole time away from work, friends, family. In the end, after a couple of weeks of looking at other meditation opportunities, I decided to take on the challenge of attending the

90-day personal retreat at Gaia House. I would start on April 1, 1998, and end in July.

Because I wasn't sure what I'd be doing after the retreat ended, I put my consulting business, Tara Associates, on hold; set up automatic payments for ongoing payables; gave my notice to vacate my apartment; sold back my leased BMW at a loss; and rented storage space for a few belongings, paintings, and my ever-faithful older Ford Taurus.

After coordinating and finalizing my three-month Gaia House visit, I started winding everything down everything in my life, reaching out to past clients and telling potential new clients that I'd be unavailable for an extended period.

I also started thinking about what I might do after the retreat. Because I was financially flush, I thought this might be an excellent opportunity for additional travel. Over the years, I'd been drawn to Tibet, India, and Nepal because of my spiritual meditation practice, and I thought it might be fun and exciting to go back to the roots of Buddhist meditation practices. I also thought about revisiting Vietnam to ask forgiveness for killing other human beings.

On March 31, 1998, I arrived at San Francisco International Airport all set for my all-night plane ride. I landed at Heathrow Airport in London very early the next morning and immediately caught a bus to Reading. From there I got on a train to Newton Abbot, the closest town to West Ogwell. Tired and excited, I got off the train around 11:30. I took a taxi to Gaia House and walked into Reception. There, I suddenly felt dazed. I'd forgotten that although we speak the same language, in England I had to listen carefully to understand what was said: the accents were that unfamiliar. I absorbed a brief and rather fast-paced overview of the house given by a young British-accented manager named Christine. She explained Gaia House rules for those sitting in silence. We were not to speak to anyone during our meditations, though we could talk to the teachers and convey essential needs to the staff via notes on a corkboard posted outside the reception office. Christine took me to my room, and I dropped off my bag and headed to the dining hall for lunch. After eating I headed back to my room, unpacked my clothes, and decided to walk around the grounds and explore this ancient house.

Set amid rolling green hills and pasture land in Devon County, Gaia House was built by wealthy landowners in approximately 1588. Various families owned the building until the mid-1920s when it became a Church of England Diocesan retreat center. In the late 1930s, it was purchased by a group of Anglican nuns, and the house became a central part of the community, providing linen goods and baked goods from their bakery. By the mid-1950s the Convent of the Companions of Jesus the Good Shepherd started expanding the main building to its current shape. The additions included a chapel (now the main meditation hall) and residential wings called the Garden Wing and Hermitage Wing. In 1996 the Gaia House Trust purchased the place after outgrowing their old building in the adjacent town of Denbury.

My first few days at Gaia House were strenuous. For one, I couldn't sleep in the provided bed because I sleep on my stomach with my feet sticking out over the end of the mattress. This bed's footboard prevented me from doing this. Additionally, I was stressed because I didn't know how to sign up for weekly meetings with a teacher—a requirement of attending a personal retreat. By the fourth day without much sleep, my sitting was already bringing up a lot of questions about why I was here and why I felt so alone and unseen because no one at the center was checking in with me. All this was building up, and I began to feel very tired and emotionally spent. Late that night, I wrote a note and left it on the manager's note board, asking if I could speak with someone about my inability to sleep in my bed and about arranging an interview with a teacher to discuss my current experience with my retreat.

Later that morning, as I headed back to the meditation hall, I saw a note for me from the managers saying that I was to meet Christopher right before lunch.

The meeting took place in the library. I sat down across from Christopher, and as soon as he said, "What's going on?" I burst into tears. He responded to my outpouring of emotion by asking, "Can you tell me what the tears are about?" I told him I couldn't sleep and that I had no idea how to schedule meetings with a teacher. I said all I knew how to do was sit, eat, do my one-hour job, and try to sleep. I told him that my experience was mostly one of being lost and sensing that no one cared to check on how I was getting on. I had thought that someone would check on me to see if I was settling in all right. Of course, as I said this, I felt childish about needing someone to check on me. After this summary, Christopher patiently told me how the house worked. He explained how to set up an appointment with a teacher once a week, and he said he would have someone take care of the bed so that I could sleep. I thanked him, and we spoke a bit about my experience with meditation practice thus far.

I told him that it was taking me at least a half hour before my mind settled down enough so that I could stay with my breath for longer than a couple of minutes. On the other hand, I was finding that my thoughts were becoming slower in speed, and despite my inability to sleep—or maybe because I hadn't been able to sleep—I sensed that my natural resistance, my wanting to know and to be in control, was breaking down. I was undergoing a letting go of sorts.

That night, I climbed into my newly configured bed and my feet easily slipped over the end of the mattress. My body heaved a big sigh of relief, and I fell right to sleep with the thought that maybe my retreat was going to happen. My ego had been cracked a bit by this challenging start. Falling asleep at last was terrific, not only because I got right to it, but because I felt inspired to get up the next morning and take my seat in the meditation hall. I was ready to take my seat.

I like having routines. When I was traveling for work, I'd find hotels with specific kinds of gym equipment and/or exciting areas to run that allowed me to carry on with my daily early morning workouts. Almost religiously I've followed these workouts with a shower, a light breakfast, and then work. Routines give me comfort.

The first routine I established at Gaia House was to rise at about 4 in the morning and sit in the Hermitage Meditation Room until the breakfast bell at 6:30. I would then eat a breakfast of oatmeal with some fruit and wash it down with tea. Next, I performed the hour of work that Gaia House required of all guests. My job was chopping vegetables for lunch, the main meal of the day. Then it was back to sitting; a walking meditation, usually at 10:30; and back to sitting until the midday meal at noon. My afternoons consisted of two two-hour sits plus two 45-minute walking meditations that I'd sandwich in before evening tea.

After tea, I might listen to the dharma talk by that night's visiting teacher. However, more often than not after tea, I would find myself sitting in my spot in the Hermitage Meditation Room until 10 or 11.

By the start of my second week, I'd established my sitting pattern, and I felt I was now taking baby steps on a path to understanding. Understanding what, I didn't know. Something just seemed to be shifting. I had no illusion that this path would be anything but long, slow, and at times challenging. So I was stunned when my second week at sitting brought a treat of sorts.

During my after-breakfast job of vegetable chopping in the kitchen, I had noticed a grey-haired, intense-looking gentleman washing breakfast dishes every day. He looked intent on doing his job well. Each cooking pot, utensil, and plate was carefully cleaned, rinsed, inspected, and placed on a rack to dry.

On this fateful day, he turned around abruptly, probably sensing that I was watching him a bit, and said in a Scottish accent; "Are you, Michael?" The noise startled me, and in a soft voice I responded, "Yes." He said, "I'm Ian, and my friend Suzie is a friend of a friend of your friend Jean. She said you'd be here at the same time as me." I immediately recalled that my best friend Jean had mentioned that a guy named Ian would be here, but in my drama of the first week, I had forgotten.

Jean, a petite, energetic, beautiful redhead who owned a Pilates studio in San Francisco, was my live-in girlfriend from 1995 to 1997. Despite our breakup, mostly because I was gone all the time, we had remained close friends. She was my closest friend. She had indeed said that the partner of a friend of a Pilates client was going to be at Gaia House at the same time I was. She had described him as an abstract artist who worked in construction and was a Scot. And here he was.

I had seen Ian in the Hermitage Meditation Room and the Dining Room as well as in the kitchen, so he wasn't unfamiliar to me. Even so, being jousted back into interacting with someone after being so engrossed in my stuff was startling.

We said "Hi" and whispered for a few minutes about how we had learned about each other—we weren't supposed to talk during our retreats—then went back to our respective jobs. Little did I know that day how much I would come to depend on Ian's strong, silent, Scottish presence to help guide me into the world of silence and introspection.

For an idea of what Ian meant to me during this retreat, here is a note that I gave him the day we said goodbye:

"To be somewhere, you've never been before can be scary, especially if some of the places you're going to are within yourself.

"What happens if I get really lost and don't know my way back? Or what if I lose my whole self? Who will understand enough about where you are to give you a hand when it is what you need and don't know how to ask? When tears begin to well from experiences or events, who will just be sitting there ready to sit or stand next to you? Who would break the talking rule with you so that you can share what a glorious day you've had or to share a deep sorrow you've uncovered? Who will point out a new path across a field?

"Whose footsteps do you hear walking down the hall to the stairwell? Who opens the door to the meditation hall? Whose jeans do you hear scraping together as they walk to their meditation spot? Who sits down next to you, adjusts their posture, then quiets down right away? Whose breathing do you hear next to yours? Who continues to show up to sit with you as you push through all the pains of sitting? Who just shows up? Who will be there?

"Who is your friend for life? To whom have you entrusted your life? In my case, it was you, Ian.

"Thank you for everything; I Love you."

The long days of sitting 10 to 15 hours in silence, interrupted only by my sore ass needing a walking break or the ringing of bells marking the moments that food was available, made my world feel very small. I was now getting up around 3 a.m., almost in a robotic manner, mindfully walking downstairs to the meditation hall, sitting until the breakfast bell rang, eating, cleaning up, chopping vegetables, then returning to the hall until 10 a.m. or so. I would then walk on the property or through the country lanes till 11 and return to the Hall to sit until the 12:30 lunch bell. Afternoons were spent meditating with one interruption for walking, stretching, and maybe a cup of tea, after which I would sit until the bell for evening tea. If I inserted any variation into in this routine, it was around this time.

Sometimes I would listen to a recorded Dharma talk from the library. Other times, I would attend a live lecture by a visiting teacher. On rare occasions, I would pick up a book in the library and open it to any page and read two to five pages to see what random lessons, thoughts, or insights the text might bring me. There were also evenings when I relaxed in the lounge, where the chairs faced tall windows facing the front lawn to the south. Here I would sit and look at the changing light as evening and night descended over the British fields outside.

My life at Gaia might sound very peaceful, especially when I was meditating, but as any person with a meditation practice might tell you, meditating can sometimes be anything but peaceful. For one, the human mind does not readily take to stillness. For another, my mind still held unresolved memories that the sitting was threatening to unearth.

For most of my adult life, my planning ability is what has made me successful at work. For years, I taught project management, and I had been an operations implementation and systems project manager. I am good at beginning a project by visualizing the end and then finding the primary path through the dependencies of each item while reviewing and understanding alternative scenarios, given that shit happens along the way. I know how to allow for variations in the course and still get to the end. It followed that my tendency to plan became an early element in my daily meditations. Once my routine had been set, my mind found itself with little on its plate to plan beyond sitting, eating, walking, sleeping, and meditating some more.

Lacking immediate new plans to devise, the planning region of my brain started to give up, and my mind shifted to reliving past events or past stories from my life. The reliving of these events was either enjoyable, or painful, or sad. I would find myself thinking about what I could have done differently or what I could have said to change the outcome of the story. I would then re-write the story in my mind, then chuckle because there was nothing I could do about a past event.

Most of these past events were painful, with only a few recollections that were positive. When previous fun events emerged, they would let me feel better about myself. When the painful ones came up, they sent me second-guessing myself. It didn't surprise me that most of the storylines that came to mind were ones I'd like to have changed.

I felt okay with watching these stories replay on the screen behind my eyes. It was natural, I knew, for my mind to go through stages of adjustment as it turned away from the actively engaged world toward a world of silence.

Chapter 21

Sounds of Silence

When I mentioned to friends that I was going on an extended silent meditation retreat, their responses were typically along the line of "I could never be silent for an hour, let alone 90 days." For many people, the thought of leaving the activity-filled and sound-filled world of their everyday life for a world of silence can be intimidating. I can relate to this fear. However, since I had already participated in many week-long and 10-day retreats, I wasn't too concerned about being silent for a longer stretch of time. What would be different was that I'd be isolated from my daily support system and I'd be a long way from home.

On the other hand, a silent retreat can be an ideal setting for people like me who genuinely love solitude and truly embrace silence but who can be distracted by the company of 20 to 100 other people meditating with me. A quote from Blaise Pascal: "All the unhappiness of men comes from one thing: Not knowing how to stay quietly in a room."

The silence in silent meditation retreats can follow different rules, depending on the teacher, the type of meditation, and the place where the retreat is taking place. In general, silence means no communication with other retreatants—no talking, no sharing written notes, even not looking directly at someone's eyes. Silence may also include a restriction on reading and even on writing one's own experiences. Because it can be important for retreatants to check in with their teachers, there are often regularly scheduled 10- to 20-minute check-in meetings.

Retreats that follow these guidelines can be very difficult for most human beings since we are genetically programmed to communicate with each other. Gaia House addresses this issue by offering a variety of retreat types, many of which include scheduled group conversations. Some of its retreats have inquiry sessions every evening, often after a dharma talk. Christopher Titmuss uses these inquiry sessions as a way for more in-depth exploration. Other retreats have regular breakout sessions that allow for discussion of experiences or specific topics. Still others, like most all Tibetan Buddhist retreats, use chanting as part of their sitting time.

A personal, solitary retreat at Gaia House means that you will have a once-a-week session with a senior teacher as a place to discuss what has come up for you during your meditations. Outside of this and possibly an occasional instruction by a retreat center manager, silence is the operative word.

Whatever mix a retreat offers, the intensely focused nature of the experience becomes an ideal opportunity for any meditator to explore her or his relationship to solitude and aloneness while also discovering a connectedness with others. Every meditator who attends a retreat soon learns that you sit alone in your particular seat. No one else sits in that spot in the universe. From this vantage point, you cannot help but understand that you are solely responsible for delivering to yourself your happiness, peace, and joy. By that same token, no one except ourselves can meet the challenging moments of heartache or loss that grace our lives.

By sitting in silence, as a member of a group, whether or not others are physically present, meditators sense that their experience echoed by every other person sitting at the retreat. Simultaneously, we are aware that we are alone in our world inside our unique view of life, that no one else experiences the world in precisely the way we do. No one shares our same past, curriculum, and path, and therefore we cannot share with anyone else the same present moment as it unfolds before us. We are alone together.

Despite distractions from people or bustle around us that can get in the way of our meditation, I believe that those of us at the retreat gain a new understanding of an essential fact: No one outside ourselves has the power to lead us into suffering. We also learn that no one but our self can release us into the realm of freedom.

Shantideva, an 8th-century Buddhist monk, and mystic said, "I was born alone and at death too, I shall die alone." I have now experienced this wisdom. Solitude allows us to explore our life as we are profoundly living it and to reconcile and accept the unique space between our birth and death.

At the same time, a silent retreat gives us an opportunity to experience this solitude while feeling our relatedness with everyone else who is sitting with us. At the same time, we grow to understand that our joys, sorrows, pains, and struggles are not unique to any one of us.

Although very subtle at times, the spirit of interconnectedness flows between each person at the retreat and between us and the world around us. We come to realize how deeply we depend on each other and everything around us.

Whenever I sat in the small Hermitage Meditation Room with two or 10 others coming and going, our connectedness was evident. I was amazed that I began to trust that others were going to show up and sit with me and I would be there for them. We never spoke, but I felt supported and dependent on them to be part of my single experience.

It did not take long for it to become clear to all of us that we had built a dynamic interconnectedness. There were moments when we were irritated with each other, moments of deep compassion, moments of indifference, and moments when someone else's actions infatuated us. Throughout all these ups and downs, in deep solitude, we found a primary connection through our silent meditation that we came to appreciate.

Milarepa, a Tibetan yogi, and poet in the late 11th century said, "Accustomed long to contemplating love and compassion, I have forgotten all difference between myself and others." This curious paradox—our aloneness versus our interrelatedness—is one that I explored on this retreat. It is a dynamic that exists in every dimension of our lives.

One question that came up for me was: Don't we all face this contradiction in our lives on almost a daily basis? To some extent, all of us suffer solitude and also crave it.

After contemplating this dynamic, I decided that I would not treat solitude and connectedness as polarizing forces but instead as a kind of duet danced by opposites. By embracing them both, I would feel at home in either universe.

My strategy worked. During my 90-day silence, I began to see the dichotomy between solitude and relatedness to others as a microcosm of all relationships. By learning to be intimate with myself, I learned how to be intimate with life and others.

So, paradoxically, it was through aloneness that I discovered completeness. I became a practitioner of the art of intimacy.

There is a popular myth that meditation pacifies us. My experience has led me to the opposite conclusion. During meditation, my body, mind, and feelings found the courage to venture toward a more profound sense of oneness. There was no need to mollify any part of me that showed up. This intimacy with the moment is, in my view, the heart of meditation. Knowing ourselves gives us stillness amidst changes and movement. It gives us silence within the noise of our thoughts and the outside world. It teaches us intimacy with all things without being hooked or captured by any one thing.

When we gain the skill of intimacy, it gives us the key to mastering life's situations. We are now free from demand, need, judgment, and expectations. We can circulate among people and be alone. We can interact with compassion, acceptance, appreciation, and forgiveness. Solitude opens our hearts.

At this point in my journey into meditation, I was wise enough to understand that the lessons of aloneness and intimacy with ourselves are not learned just once. They get repeated over and over again with every new moment. We are continually learning not to abandon a thought because, in our view, it is unspiritual, imperfect, or unworthy. We become eternal students of each moment, practicing a gentle curiosity about how we view the world and how we engage in it.

To be clear, the practice of meditation is much more than a technique or a formula. Yes, there are techniques to assist in the process of reflection. While equipped with these tools, each meditator then aims to understand, on their own, what it means to be free. I'm not implying being free from responsibility, commitment, or integrity. I'm speaking about the freedom of not being imprisoned, confined, or governed by an exterior or internal force. Each of us discovers this freedom alone.

Fear will always come into the picture during this quest. Sometimes it is the fear of reliving painful events. Sometimes it's our fear of what is going to happen next. More often than not, we fear not making the "right" choices. It is almost as if we want the world to come with guarantees about what will happen next in our life. During meditation, people will also touch a deep fear of being no one, nothing to anyone, including ourselves. And, of course, there is the fear of having nothing.

FEAR, as we have seen, is often an acronym for False Experience Appearing Real, or False Expectations Appearing Real. When we examine fear, we often learn that it is the result of other emotions, for example Greed, the fear of not having enough. Anger, the fear of being hurt. Anxiety, the fear of uncertainty. Or jealousy, the fear of somehow being less than someone else.

If we look at these fears with open curiosity, we can harness them to help guide our freedom. It is not easy to befriend FEAR because doing so brings us closer to uncertainty, the unknown, which creates anxiety. And anxiety is usually viewed as an unpleasant aggregate.

One last thought on silence. There is a common pitfall that those of us who follow the path of meditation run into while on the journey towards freedom, and that is: Taking refuge from ourselves by submerging ourselves in somebody else's life, by co-opting another person's identity. We can run into this phenomenon by holding someone, say a teacher or a guru, as a savior who is going to rescue us. Conversely, it can also happen if we hold ourselves up as the savior of someone else. Neither path leads to freedom but instead to become a prisoner of fear, our own or someone else's.

I am grateful that for me, silence has become a friend, a solace, and a vehicle for bringing all my stuff to the forefront to look at, embrace and accept.

Chapter 22

Seeing

As the hours, days, and weeks of the retreat slipped by; silence became my home. Eruptions of bliss, joy, sorrow, pain, and distractions all became my friends, as did my fear of not being enough, not having enough, and not being. There were also times when my mind wanted to distract itself from inquiry and silence so that I could ignore the mirror of myself.

One morning I had a revolution in my stoic thinking, quite by accident. The day began with a kind of prelude to what was to become later in the day, a concert of songs from my past. After breakfast, during my vegetable chopping, I got distracted by a sound in my head, which turned into a Beatles song: "You Won't See Me" from the *Rubber Soul* album. I'm not sure if it was the title or a memory of a high school girlfriend who suddenly stopped seeing me some 30 years ago, that spun my mind into internally singing this song.

When I left the kitchen and headed to my cushion in the Hermitage Meditation Hall, "You Won't See Me" kept playing over and over in my head and did not stop when I eased myself onto the cushion. I allowed the space for this musical interlude to exist in my mind, and it suddenly transitioned to the next song on the album, "Nowhere Man," a favorite Beatle song, and then the next, "Think for Yourself."

With these three titles, I wondered if I was giving myself a message. I let myself continue singing *Rubber Soul* songs in my head until I went through the whole album a couple of times. Then I moved logically onto the subsequent album, *Revolver,* my all-time favorite Beatles album. Starting with "Taxman" and ending with "Tomorrow Never Knows," the songs tripped right off my brain in order, just as my old bandmate Jim G. and I would sing them back in high school when we'd practice in his bedroom. Hour after hour, we'd sing these songs, both of us playing our guitars and harmonizing. Although we eventually joined a band called "The Rosscarbery Express" (named after a town in Ireland because the drummer was Irish, and it was his band), Jim and I never lost the joy of singing Beatles songs together in the afternoons.

One thing was sure as I sat in silence while The Beatles played in my head. The lyrics of many of their songs spoke to me in a fun, profound, and prophetic ways. Then, as quickly as this songfest started, the music ended poignantly with "Tomorrow Never Knows" just as the bell in the steeple tower rang out boldly for lunch.

By now, eight weeks into the retreat, my sitting schedule was firmly set. Occasionally, I'd get up at 2:00 or 2:30 a.m. instead of 3, after about three- or four-hours' sleep, I seemed to be requiring a lot less sleep these days, maybe because there was little for my mind to process during sleep. I was sleeping anywhere from three to five hours a night, and all my rest seemed to be solidly rooted with very little dreaming.

On the following morning, Sunday, June 7, 1998, as I headed to my cushion in the meditation hall, I was struck by how almost timeless everything seemed to be. I was merely here, and nothing else seemed to exist.

Then an astounding event commenced its unfolding. About 5:00 a.m., I got up from my cushion and decided to head outside to see what the day held for me. The pattern of leaving the meditation hall was a change from my usual routine; I almost always sat until the morning breakfast bell. On this day, however, there was a lightness in me and everything around me. It was the feeling of being skinless, without borders, and I was becoming curious about my being more awake now, and I wanted to look out at the world.

With the meditation door slowly closing behind me, I slipped my jacket on and stepped through the building door and into the crisp early morning. Standing at the top of the driveway, I looked out to see the crease of a dawning light outlining the hill-filled horizon. I sensed the wholeness of the world around and inside me, and to ground myself I began to do some walking meditation in the upper driveway.

About half an hour later, the sky lightened a little more, and I headed down the driveway, paying close attention to the overall sense of everything, and the coolness of the early summer morning air on my cheeks and hands. The stillness of the dawning day, the smell of wet grass, and the sense of clarity left me noting that I was merely walking down the driveway.

At its base, I turned right and headed down the country lane. The asphalt was moist with the night's dew, and small puddles glistened with the partial moonlight dancing off their surfaces. Slowly moving down the road, as if I didn't want to disturb the morning air, I looked over to my left and saw some cows in the field with their heads bent toward the ground. I could hear them breathe as they moved slowly through the ankle-high grass. The noise of their chewing gave me a feeling of warmth.

About 20 yards farther down the lane, I saw one cow's head sticking through the barbed wire fence that bordered the field and road. As I approached this one, I couldn't help noticing that one of its eyes was infected and swollen. There was the sound of buzzing flies near the infection, but the cow didn't seem to mind. The other eye was perfectly fine.

I noted that I didn't feel any sense of aversion to the infected eye, or an attraction to seeing that the other eye was healthy. The infected eye was infected, and the healthy eye was healthy. Raising my head to expand my view away from the cow, the realization hit me that nothing was "better" or "worse" than anything else. Everything was the same, although different. I felt an intense openness as if the membrane between the rest of the world and me were giving way to nothing. It was as if everything that separated me from the world around was being peeled away.

I took another couple of steps, then stopped and looked up and over to my right across a field toward the dawning sun creeping up above the rolling frost-painted hills. As I looked out past the trees, I felt an immense sense of wholeness. It was as if someone had taken a glass cover off the world around me and exposed everything to itself and me with embodied crystal clarity. The veil of me (with all my stuff) was gone. The cloud of unknowing dissipated like the dawning of the day, of life. There wasn't anything out there, and I didn't exist. It just was one thing, life.

There weren't any feelings or thoughts per se that accompanied this experience, just a quiet peacefulness and a sense that I was both in and of the world at the same time, and nothing and everything existed. I felt as if I'd awakened from a long sleep.

I (though "I" is an inaccurate descriptive term for me at this moment, as there seemed to be no I) stood in complete, humbled awe of this experience. The sheer sense of oneness was by itself fluidly transfixing. The entity I had perceived as self, seemed to be coming apart. This breaking down of the "I" reached the point where "I" didn't exist.

As this experience unfolded, my thoughts seemed to have difficulty using the word "I" as if it suggested a false reference to anything that existed. My consciousness was sensing rather than thinking that everything is made up of me and I was made up of everything.

Just seeing this way, without a particular thought in mind, allowed everything to be perfect. Nothing meant anything more or less than anything else. All was the same; all were distinct, all was perfect as it is. Part of what was transpiring was that I was placing light attention on what I was doing at the moment and no attention to what I would be doing later or what I'd done in the past. This level of presence allowed for a new level of understanding of what is.

The morning breakfast bell rang in the near distance, and the sound seemed to dance through the air and bounce off the hills. This break in the silence of the morning dawn didn't stop my sense of oneness. The sound only seemed to partner with the world.

I made my way back toward the house slowly and methodically, wondering if I would be jostled out of my sense of being awakened to things as they are.

Yes, the clear sense and understanding of that morning's events faded in and out over the rest of that day and the days that followed. However, something extraordinary happened to me that morning: a permanent shift in understanding and knowledge of the world and of life and what it means to be a human being. I felt that I had awakened from a deep, hypnotic sleep. My perceptions of what self-was and what I was, had unraveled. It was humbling, sad, yet blissful.

This sensation was sheathed in the clear understanding and knowledge that I could never un-learn, un-see, and un-know the truth of life at this moment as it is. I realized that I would not always be able to get out of my way to see things as they are, but I would be able to find my way back to see things as they are if I wanted to.

Chapter 23

Transitioning from Silence

About 5 o'clock on the following Thursday morning, after a walking meditation, I began to feel a little panicky. I was experiencing the falling-away of my previous version of the truth and world. The veneers were slipping off, and nothing was coming forth to replace them. I was experiencing the sensation of losing "me," or what I thought was me. I didn't understand what was going on because the previous place from which I operated in the world was disappearing. I was uncomfortable.

My predicament reminded me of a recurring childhood dream. In that dream, I'd drop into a vast, empty vast nothingness where everything seemed to exist even though nothing was there. Then came a sensation of peace, with everything perfect at that moment. As I looked out of my own eyes, I would see me and simultaneously the limitless world.

This childhood dream was both frightful and peaceful because every sensory medium, especially light and sound, seemed to smash together into one vast vacuum.

It was bright, loud, and silent and dark all at the same time. But because I'd always wake up to find my "me," the child, again, I didn't spend a lot of time thinking about the dream afterward.

Because of my recent experience, however, it seemed appropriate to revisit this memory.

For me now, the feeling of non-self was the same yet very different. It wasn't something from which I could wake up. It was constant and more than a little overwhelming. I started trying to push the vast space of nothing away. My growing fear (there's that word again) was that I'd soon be going home and would have to deal with the world, people, family, and friends with little or no idea who I was or what I'd be in their presence. My anxiety about my state of mind was causing me to sabotage my most recent meditations as I succumbed to the chatter of my questions.

I knew I needed guidance. I made an interview appointment with Christina Feldman, my primary teacher during the 90-day retreat. We met just after lunch. As soon as I began telling her what was going on and what had happened the previous Sunday, I burst into tears. After the sobbing ended and I finally got out the rest of the story, Christina looked at me calmly and said, "This is great! You're just losing self." This statement was not reassuring. I became even more panicky. "Then who will I be?" I asked. She responded, "Your 'I' will still be there, just not in the same way."

A slow smile began to creep across my face as a realization sank in, that in a way I was dying. My mind, the operating system for the being called Michael, would know how to take care of the things necessary for me to exist in the world, and Michael (me with additional insights) would have different options and ways of transacting and behaving in the world.

Christina went on to say, "You can trust your perceptions. If you let go of the fear of not knowing who you are, you will find that there is nothing to be afraid of."

Her statement struck me right in the heart, and new tears fell from my eyes. She then ended our discussion by saying, with a big smile, "This is good."

A snippet from my notes:

After meeting with Christina yesterday, I am feeling better about everything. While in the Dining Hall at lunch today with 30 + people eating, I tuned into the sound of lunch. It was extraordinary. I found myself listening to the music of the meal by hearing people move from getting their food, to eating it, to the noise of chairs on the floor as people left the tables. Hearing all this with the clarity of just what it was. There were no value judgments in my awareness nor were there any reasons to shift from this hearing and seeing. It was the first time it was comfortable to be in this space while being around other people.

Sitting there listening to this cacophony of exquisite noises called lunch, I recalled a remark that I'd heard once, although I don't know who the author is: "Self-righteousness is the biggest obstacle man has to overcome to become free. That is why self-righteousness is known as the fiercest obstacle at the innermost temple door."

Tonight, as I sit in my room, the thoughts I'm having as I write, are: Anything added to the words "I am" is limiting and separating. And if I say I am "experiencing" something, does that mean I am re-touching a past event or am I genuinely experiencing something new?

From what I was learning, it appears that all conflict in the world is caused by there being an "I" to hold on to and embrace. If I was valuing my "I" more than another person's "I", what I'd be doing was, thinking there is something wrong with another person's version of the world. I could be deciding my version is better. It is only better for me and no one else, therefore how could it be better than another's? Everyone has their curriculum.

My time on this 90-day retreat was coming to an end. It had changed me permanently. For the rest of my life, I will be affected by having grown to understand myself more deeply, by becoming aware that my separate self is one with all of us, and by having seen "what is." The experience both challenged and engaged me. Of course, there isn't a me, so I cannot lay claim to a "new me."

Because Ian was scheduled to leave two days before I did, we were slowly reintroduced together into the world outside of Gaia House. Christina suggested a couple of ways for us to make the transition.

First, we would participate in another group retreat that was just five days long. Second, we would make accompanied trips to the towns of Totnes and Newton Abbot.

During these trips, we'd go to a café and maybe have tea. We would also join one of the Gaia House managers on a journey to town to buy supplies for the center. These two-hour-long trips would allow us to ramp up our slow, methodical and non-talking ways of participating in the world to a more active form of being.

Ian and I took three such trips, two to Totnes and one to Newton Abbot. Our first trip was filled with open-eyed wonder. We had tea and breakfast, and we stared at all the purposed activity in the café. The noise of people talking with each other about all sorts of stuff was almost overwhelming. By our third trip, Ian and I had gotten used to all the visual and verbal activity and even participated in it by engaging with some people.

Another of Christina's suggestions was to participate in the sitting and walking meditations that the five-day retreat group would be doing in its last couple of days. The length of these meditations was 45 minutes, quite a change from the two- to three-hour stretches that we had been doing.

These two activities helped to ease me toward the day that I would be leaving. I certainly needed the transitional time. Gaia House had been my home for three months, and it had given me a place to discover my life. I felt a deep sadness at the prospect of leaving. The 90 days had been the most rewarding experience of my life, and the lessons from it will carry me all the way to my death.

On the last day of the five-day retreat, there was a "go-around" during which the retreat participants shared their experience with the group. When the retreat leader asked if anyone wanted to start speaking, there was a pause, then Ian spoke up and said he'd like to be the first to go. His story was beautiful.

"When I woke up this morning," he recounted, "all I heard was, I'm going from nothing into nothing, from nowhere into nowhere. I finally got up out of bed though I didn't know who I was. I went outside for a walk, and there was nothing outside. There was nothing there." His voice was shaking as he spoke, I began to cry. It was profoundly moving to hear him talk about his morning.

After Ian finished, there was silence for two or three minutes. Then I stood up and spoke. I acknowledged that I had learned more than I ever thought I would, most of all that we are all one. I said that I still wanted to learn more about who I was, and I asked for their help. Would everyone look at me for a couple of minutes, so I could look at each of them and see the parts of me that I, by myself, couldn't experience? They did, and it was a wonderful experience. Witnessing the sameness and differences in everyone from myself was sublime.

My departure date was now two days away. On Tuesday, June 30, 1998, I was driven to Totnes. I had lunch with Gretchen, a kitchen manager, and Christine, the manager who signed me in when I arrived for my retreat. Finding out more about them was fun. Gretchen was born in New York, was smart as a whip and still had the New York accent and speed of conversation. She was engaged to a man who had been a Buddhist monk and had disrobed. Christine, from England, was sweet and softspoken. She had particpated in retreats all over Europe and decided to come to Gaia House as reception manager so she could consider what she would be doing next.

Seeing them day-to-day and not being able to speak with them had been difficult, but now that I got to talk, I was delighted to hear some of their stories and how they ended up working at Gaia House. Gretchen had started attending meditation retreats in various places including India; she planned to settle down in Totnes and start a yoga studio after she completed her year of volunteering as kitchen manager at Gaia House. Although Christine hadn't figured out what was next for her, she knew that traveling would probably be on her agenda. After lunch, I walked around town for a while. Then we drove back to Gaia House so I could say goodbye to Ian, who was leaving that afternoon.

On Wednesday, my full last day at Gaia House, I did my usual morning of sitting and walking meditations. After breakfast, I chopped my final batch of vegetables with a little bit of sorrow—I loved working in the kitchen—thoroughly cleaned my room, ate lunch, walked to Newton Abbot and had tea, and then came back to pack up my belongings. That night, there were just three of us sitting in the large main meditation room. Just before the end of the sitting time, I got up, walked to the front of the room, and rang the singing bowl to signal the end of the evening's meditation. It was a symbolic acknowledgment that my stay had ended. After that, I went outside and walked around the building in the moonlit night thinking, remembering, wondering, and then silently said goodbye.

Chapter 24

Postscript

My three months at Gaia House have come and gone. It is early August 1998, nine and a half years after I stood on the edge of a cliff in Big Sur, ready to jump into the abyss and die because I wanted to be free. I wanted to be free of the binds, limitations, and beliefs that reflected my struggle to live this life. I sought to fall into freedom, and I got my wish. Only I fell into the freedom of life, not death.

I am preparing for my next adventure, an around-the-world trip, inspired by the principles I've discovered over the past ten years. The journey will start with a weeklong meditation at Gaia House in England to reconnect with my path. Then I'll head to Sweden to sightsee and visit a friend in Stockholm before a week in Hamburg, Germany, with another dear friend whom I met during my previous stay at Gaia House.

Then the adventurous segment of my trip will begin. From Germany, I will fly to Asia, where I expect to spend six months walking through the northern parts of

India, Nepal, Tibet, and Thailand. My last stop will be Vietnam, where I will commemorate my thirtieth anniversary of fighting there as a soldier. I want this trip to Vietnam to be about love and forgiveness.

Back in 1989 when the process of falling started, if you were to glance at me and my life, the veneer looked great. But if you had looked under it, you would have seen that I was failing at almost all my intimate relationships, I was miserable, and filled with sadness and despair. Back then, I knew that if I kept on doing what I was doing, I would get more of what I was getting, and what I was getting was not appealing.

Standing on the Big Sur cliff, I decided to do whatever it took to find a path to freedom. My goals were internal peace, compassion, and enough desire to live to continue to be a contributor to humanity.

I gave up the home I lived in, slept in my car, gave away most of my possessions, and stripped my life down to the bare essentials. My path included seeing therapists, going to seminars aimed at cracking my veneer, reading many books, and spending more than a thousand hours sitting in meditation and silence.

Falling into Freedom is my story about how I found a way to embrace living. Everybody's story is different. I struggled with my hard-headed nature and my resistance to being swayed by other people's recommendations. However, I do think that anyone looking for personal freedom will find the five principles I've outlined here to be helpful tools in a path to freedom.

I cannot suggest that anyone use or follow my particular path to freedom. As the Buddha said: "We ourselves must walk the path." However, one component of my road and Buddha's that I can recommend to everybody is meditation.

A regular meditation practice can become a vehicle for self-inquiry for any person set on mindful change. Yes, transition is difficult for any person. Meditation will always make it more doable.

My 90-day meditation retreat taught me that I am not who I thought I was. I was able to let "thought" go and learn a fantastic truth, that I do not exist to fight life. I live purely to unfold into life. Even today, the more I stay present, the more I understand about myself and the world around me. For this, I thank the teachers, past and present, in my life. I am particularly grateful to Jack Kornfield, Christopher Titmuss, and of course, Christina Feldman.

During my stay at Gaia House, I discovered joy where there had previously seemed to be none. This awakening to joy came from opening my mind to seeing reality in different ways. I got to see how my mind works. I saw how experience becomes thought that then determines actions. This new dimension of understanding allowed me to see how some of my "patterned sufferings" were merely behavioral structures that I was continuing to reinforce through thought.

Now I can see through the process that my mind had been using to react to events. It would immediately wrap a belief structure around my reaction to something, and that belief structure then dictated my actions. My mind has since learned to consider alternative responses and answers. It now allows new information to enter not as set truths but as possibilities. Before, my ego created a false sense of reality based on past thoughts and fear. Now I know that those thoughts don't exist in nature and therefore don't exist in me.

During my fall into freedom, I worked on not identifying with any one thing or thought because doing so would perpetuate my separateness. I practiced shifting my attention away from thoughts about the past because the past cannot determine the present, and I practiced letting go of thought entirely, which freed me to feel myself unfolding and evolving.

I became particularly aware of how accessible meditation can be in my daily life. In the final two and a half weeks of my long retreat, I realized that it is possible to see everything as perfect, just as it is, at that moment. Seeing something like this without attaching a particular thought to it makes that thing perfect as it is. This depth of understanding became possible only when I stayed present. I have also felt the undoing of what I perceived as "self" to the point where at times "I" didn't seem to exist.

The practice of meditation allows us the opportunity to free thoughts from past entanglements. Simple, quiet, open attention will enable us to be in the moment, to see what is, and to open the doors of awareness and emptiness. In this place of being, resides all truth.

Krishnamurti said. "Meditation is one of the most extraordinary things, and if you do not know what it is, you are like the blind man in a world of bright color, shadows and moving light. It is not an intellectual affair, but when the heart enters into the mind, the mind has quite a different quality; it is really, then, limitless, not only in its capacity to think, to act efficiently, but also in its sense of living in a vast space where you are part of everything."

Also, "Meditation is the movement of love…"

Keeping the channels of awareness open will be my continued challenge. I have promised myself that whenever I feel the urge to ask myself the questions, who am I? Why am I here? What is the meaning of life? I will do so with openness and curiosity instead of pushing them away. I would like to remember Milarepa's comment, "A wandering thought is the essence of wisdom."

Every day now is filled with opportunities to see clearly. Regardless of what I've learned about myself and freedom, I know that freedom isn't a place to arrive at or go to. It is an evolving flow of moments wherein my curriculum is presented to me. My Five Principles of Freedom will serve me as questions I will continue to ask myself until the end of my life:

1. Can I continue to forgive myself and others?
2. Can I not identify with a pre-conceived version of "self"?
3. Can I not base my thought and actions on attachments or aversions arising from the self?
4. Can I let go of my past actions, thoughts, and events so that now is seen clearly?
5. Can I accept what is?

Today and each moment, as I work on waking up to address what is in front of me on my quest to be free; I keep in mind my new version of a Zen lesson on enlightenment:

"Before freedom, chop wood carry water; after freedom, chop wood carry water..."

About the Author

Michael Doud is an explorer of both the inner and outer worlds of his life. Never did he think as a 6-year-old boy standing on the sand in Redondo Beach, CA that he would travel the world. Michael has explored Tibet, Europe, India, North America, Nepal, Mexico, China, and other Asian countries discovering how the people, cultures, and belief structures of these countries are both similar and different from his own.

Along the way, he discovered that this was only an appetizer to real exploration. He learned that the more fascinating and deeper adventure was learning about how his mind, actions, and behavior responded to work, relationships, killing, love, addiction, family, homelessness, parenting, and depression. From the cultural explosion brought forth by the protests and love-ins of the 1960s to sitting in silence for ninety days in an old English convent in 1998; *Falling into Freedom* is his journey to discover his five principles for personal freedom. These principles have assisted him to see things as they are and not how he wanted them to be.

Book Listing

Book Name & Author

NAME OF BOOK	AUTHOR
Emptiness Dancing	Adyashanti
The Impact of Awakening	Adyashanti
As A Man Thinketh	James Allen
The Bridge Across Forever	Richard Bach
Jonathan Livingston Seagull	Richard Bach
Illusions	Richard Bach
Running from Safety	Richard Bach
One	Richard Bach
Initiation Human and Solar	Alice A. Bailey
The Essential Rumi	Colman Barks
The Soul of Rumi	Colman Barks
Buddhism Without Beliefs	Stephen Batchelor
Verses from the Center	Stephen Batchelor
After Buddhism	Stephen Batchelor
Everyday Sacred	Sue Bender
Heartwood of the Bodhi Tree	Buddhadasa Bhikkhu
Transitions	William Bridges
What Should I Do with My Life	Po Bronson
The Secret	Rhonda Byrne
The Teachings of Don Juan	Carlos Castaneda
A Separate Reality	Carlos Castaneda
Journey to Ixtlan	Carlos Castaneda
The Active Side of Infinity	Carlos Castaneda

NAME OF BOOK	AUTHOR
Tales of Power	Carlos Castaneda
The Power of Silence	Carlos Castaneda
The Turning Point	Fritjof Capra
Finite and Infinite Games	James P. Carse
everything arises, everything falls away	Ajahn Chah
When Things Fall Apart	Pema Chodren
Ageless Body, Timeless Mind	Deepak Chopra
Quantum Healing	Deepak Chopra
The Man Who Tapped the Secrets of the Universe	Glenn Clark
The Alchemist	Paulo Coelho
By the River Piedra I Sat Down and Wept	Paulo Coelho
The Zahir: A Novel of Obsession	Paulo Coelho
The Valkyries	Paulo Coelho
The Seven Habits of Highly Effective People	Stephen R. Covey
The Right Use of Will	Ceanne DeRohan
The Tibetan Book of the Dead (translated by)	Gyurme Dorje
The Power of Intention	Dr. Wayne Dyer
The Quiet Mind	White Eagle
You are Becoming Galactic Human	Virginia Essene & Sheldon Nidle
The Little Prince	Antone De Saint-Exupery
Stories of the Spirit, Stories of the Heart	Christina Feldman & Jack Kornfield
Silence	Christina Feldman
First Directions: Meditation	Christina Feldman
Thorsons Principles of Meditation	Christina Feldman
Living in the Heart	Paul Ferrini

NAME OF BOOK	AUTHOR
Reflections of the Christ Mind	Paul Ferrini
The Science of Being	Eugene Fersen
A Course in Miracles	Foundation for Inner Peace
When Fear Falls Away	Jan Frazier
The Prophet	Kahlil Gibran
Eat Pray Love	Elizabeth Gilbert
Blink	Malcolm Gladwell
The Tipping Point	Malcolm Gladwell
Instructions to the Cook	Bernard Glassman
Bearing Witness	Bernard Glassman
Seeking the Heart of Wisdom	Joseph Goldstein & Jack Kornfield
Peace is Every Step	Thich Nhat Hanh
Living Buddha, Living Christ	Thich Nhat Hanh
Zen in the Art of Archery	Eugen Harrigel
The Last Days of Ancient Sunlight	Thom Hartman
Power vs. Force	David R. Hawkins M.D. – Ph. D.
Choices	Shad Helmstetter
Siddhartha	Herman Hesse
Conscious Evolution	Barbara Marx Hubbard
The Robots' Rebellion	David Icke
He	Robert Johnson
She	Robert Johnson
We	Robert Johnson
Inner Work	Robert Johnson
Balancing Heaven and Earth	Robert Johnson

NAME OF BOOK	AUTHOR
Wheels of Life	Anodea Judith
Full Catastrophe Living	Jon Kabat-Zinn Ph.D.
Wherever You Go, There You Are	Jon Kabat-Zinn Ph.D.
Coming to Our Senses	Jon Kabat-Zinn Ph.D.
Loving What Is	Byron Katie
The Future of Love	Daphne Rose Kingman
The Crystal Stair	Eric Klein
The Inner Door (Volume 1)	Eric Klein
The Inner Door (Volume 2)	Eric Klein
A Path with Heart	Jack Kornfield
After the Ecstasy, the Laundry	Jack Kornfield
The Wise Heart	Jack Kornfield
Bringing Home the Dharma	Jack Kornfield
Teachings of the Buddha (Edited by)	Jack Kornfield
Krishnamurti: Reflections of the Self	Krishnamurti
Meditations	Krishnamurti
The Age of Spiritual Machines	William Kurzweil
We, The Arcturians	Dr. Norma Milanovich
Tao Te Ching	Stephen Mitchell
The Enlightened Mind	Stephen Mitchell
The Essence of Wisdom	Stephen Mitchell
Mutant Message Down Under	Maria Morgan
Care of the Soul	Thomas Moore
The Upanishads Part 1 & Part 2 (Translated by)	F. Max Muller
The Bhagavad Gita (Translated by, or by)	Swami Nikhilananda Swami Prabhupada

NAME OF BOOK	AUTHOR
The Dance	Oriah Mountain Dreamer
The Invitation	Oriah Mountain Dreamer
What We Ache For	Oriah Mountain Dreamer
Ramana Maharshi	Arthur Osborne
Illuminations	Stephen C. Paul & Gary Max Collion
Road Less Traveled	Scott Peck
The Patchwork of Self-Transformation	Eva Pierrakos
Zen and the Art of Motorcycle Maintenance	Robert M. Pirsig
Lila: An Inquiry into Morals	Robert M. Pirsig
The Celestine Prophecy	James Redfield
The Tibetan Book of Living and Dying	Sogyal Rinpoche
Faith: Trusting Your Own Deepest Experience	Sharon Salzberg
Loving Kindness	Sharon Salzberg
The Future of Love	Sharon Salzberg
Heal Thy Self	Saki Santorelli

Mother, a trilogy
   I The Divine Materialism
   II The New Species
   III The Mutation of Death
	Satprem

The Spirit of Loving (Edited by)	Emily Hilburn Sell
Transformers	Jacquelyn Small
Dark Night of the Soul	St. John of the Cross
Life and Teaching of the Masters of the Far East (Volumes 1 – 6)	Baird T. Spalding
The Passion of the Western Mind	Richard Tarnas
The Heart of Buddhist Meditation	Nyanaponika Thera

NAME OF BOOK	AUTHOR
The Green Buddha	Christopher Titmuss
Light on Enlightenment	Christopher Titmuss
The Power of Now	Eckhart Tolle
A New Earth	Eckhart Tolle
The Cloud of Unknowing and other Works	Unknown – Intro by Clifton Wolters
River of Fire, River of Water	Taitetsu Unno
Conversations With God – Book 1	Neale Donald Walsh
Book 2	
Book 3	
The New Revelations	Neale Donald Walsh
Love & Awakening	John Welwood
Journey of the Heart	John Welwood
The Heart Aroused	David Whyte
No Boundaries	Ken Wilber
Integral Psychology	Ken Wilber
A Brief History of Everything	Ken Wilber
Whispering Winds of Change	Stuart Wilde
The Force	Stuart Wilde
Sixth Sense	Stuart Wilde
Return to Love	Marianne Williamson
The Healing of America	Marianne Williamson
MAP – Medial Assistance Program	Machaelle Small Wright
Autobiography of a Yogi	Paramahansa Yogananda
The Art of Possibility	Rosamund & Benjamin Zander